LITTLE HOUSE ON THE PRAIRIE

A Reader's Companion

TWAYNE'S MASTERWORK STUDIES

Robert Lecker, General Editor

LITTLE HOUSE ON THE PRAIRIE

A Reader's Companion

Virginia L. Wolf
University of Wisconsin–Stout

TWAYNE PUBLISHERS
An Imprint of Simon & Schuster Macmillan
New York

PRENTICE HALL INTERNATIONAL
London Mexico City New Delhi Singapore Sydney Toronto

Twayne's Masterwork Studies No. 164

Little House on the Prairie: A Reader's Companion
Virginia L. Wolf

Twayne Publishers
An Imprint of Simon & Schuster Macmillan
1633 Broadway
New York, NY 10019

Library of Congress Cataloging-in-Publication Data

Wolf, Virginia L.
    Little house on the Prairie ; American myth / by Virginia L. Wolf.
      p.   cm. — (Masterworks studies ; 164)
    Includes bibliographical references and index.
    ISBN 0-8057-8820-4 (cloth). — ISBN 0-8057-8821-2 (paper)
    1. Wilder, Laura Ingalls, 1867–1957. Little house on the prairie.
    2. Wilder, Laura Ingalls, 1867–1957—Criticism and interpretation.
    3. Women and literature—United States—History—20th century.
    4. Children's stories, American—History and criticism. 5. Frontier and pioneer life in literature. 6. Myth in literature. I. Title.
    II. Series: Twayne's masterwork studies ; no. 164.
    PS3545.I342L58   1996
    813'.52—dc20   96-31197
                                         CIP

10 9 8 7 6 5 4 3 2 1 (hc)
10 9 8 7 6 5 4 3 2 1 (pbk)

Printed in the United States of America

For My Family

*For Strelsa and Harry Bonham—Mom and Dad—who reared
me very near the little house on the prairie; and for Carol,
especially, who taught me how to love both little houses and the
prairie and gave me the time to write this book; but also for Marty
and Rita, members of my new "family," who supported me during
the latter stages of writing this book*

Contents

Preface

I owe a huge debt to Laura Ingalls Wilder. My work on the *Little House* books has always come at times when they have had rich meaning for me. My first writing was about *Little House in the Big Woods* as an evocation of a peaceful, timeless, serene, beautiful Wisconsin winter as part of a loving family. It expressed all the joy I was finding in my new home in Eau Claire, Wisconsin. Next I turned to the use of "center" and "circle" in the *Little House* books as metaphors for a secure but vital relationship between the self and the world—a healthy balance. This paper grew out of a time when I was experiencing a terrific burst of creativity and productivity, made possible, I believe, by a long period of stability at home and at work. Shortly thereafter, I began to undergo a prolonged transition, beginning with the adolescence of our son, David. While he struggled to achieve independence and I tried to let go as much as seemed reasonable, I was thankful for having the *Little House* books to read again, especially thankful for their serenity and wisdom about being able to control only oneself—not others or nature.

Now, reading and writing about *Little House on the Prairie* over the course of the last two years has led me back to a book I read much earlier, Alan Watts's *The Wisdom of Insecurity*.[1] My life has been increasingly insecure over the past ten years. Change has been the order of the day: our youngest child's departure for college, the "empty nest syndrome," a six-year stint as an administrator, menopause and other signs of age, my return to the classroom and writing, beginning a master's of divinity program, the death of my partner's grandmother and mother, the sale of our home of 18 years, a cohousing project with another couple, and the wedding of our daughter Laura (on 21 October 1995). But, as is true of Wilder's books, below the surface of all this change a current of joy and serenity has run. Never before have I experienced periods of rapid change with so little anxiety. These days, like Laura Ingalls, I feel "all excited inside . . . [because I] never know what will happen next, nor where . . . [I'll] be tomorrow" (*LHP*, 327).[2]

Little House on the Prairie never lies about the existence of fear, suffering, and loss, but it shows us that there are also peace, beauty, and love. As I will try to show, the novel's wisdom and serenity arise from Laura's basic trust in life, a trust she acquires from feeling unconditionally loved by Pa and Ma. She knows deep within, well below the level of consciousness, that her parents would do anything necessary to ensure her survival, and she experiences them as consistently capable of performing whatever actions are needed for the family's welfare. They are people who care deeply, and therefore they rear a daughter who also cares deeply. It is in her caring for places, people, objects, events, and words that we encounter Laura Ingalls Wilder.

Writings about the *Little House* books typically emphasize that these books capture the pioneer experience. As we will see, this was Wilder's intention. She knew that she was writing about a lost way of life and wanted to offer her experience—the pioneer experience of this country—to children. Some writers focus on her portrait of a sturdy family's participation in taming the west. Others write of the Ingallses' living in harmony with the wilderness. These two readings may seem contradictory, but I want to give credit to both, since they reflect the ambivalence and ambiguity of these books and of American myth.[3] As many scholars of our history and culture have noted, we have long held and still hold conflicting views of nature, seeing it as both sacred and demonic. Likewise, we both idealize and demonize American civilization and one of its chief instruments, technology. In fact, the American mind seems to be characterized by conflict between opposing views. This might be criticized as indecision, but it might also be considered an accurate reflection of the complexity of reality and a more appropriate response than either view alone could ever be.

As I intend to show in this study, such conflict runs throughout *Little House on the Prairie* and Wilder's other books.[4] Had she not deeply cherished her childhood and grieved deeply over its loss—and the eventual loss of Pa, Ma, and Mary—we would not have the books in which that childhood will live forever. Her combined delight and sorrow produce the distinctive tone of her books. She reassures us serenely that, although often frightening, difficult, or sad, everything young Laura experiences is fascinating and valuable—worth evoking in vivid and abundant detail. This tone evinces her caring, not only about her childhood but also about the children who will be her readers. Moreover, to begin writing her story at age 62 must have been—at the very least—extremely difficult. Wilder needed to learn much of her craft from her daughter, Rose Wilder Lane; and this too can be seen as a source of conflict. Lane would use some of her mother's material to write her own books, and although she felt compelled to help her mother, she resented the time that editing the *Little House* books took away from her own writing career.[5]

Strong feelings, then, must have motivated Wilder during the 13 years it took to produce these books. These feelings in all their many colors and nuances—especially the need to remember and preserve what is gone—provide the undercurrents to which I have responded. The complexity, strength, confidence, and commitment they convey keep me returning to the books time and time again.

Acknowledgments

Material from the Rose Wilder Lane papers at the Herbert Hoover Presidential Library, West Branch, Iowa, used with permission of Abagail MacBride.

Material and illustrations from *Little House on the Prairie,* text copyright 1935 by Laura Ingalls Wilder, copyright © renewed 1963 by Roger L. MacBride; pictures copyright 1953 by Garth Williams, copyright © renewed 1981 by Garth Williams. Material from *Little House in the Big Woods,* text copyright 1932 by Laura Ingalls Wilder; copyright renewed 1960 by Roger L. MacBride. From *On the Banks of Plum Creek,* text copyright 1937 by Laura Ingalls Wilder, renewed © 1963 by Roger L. MacBride. Reprinted by permission of HarperCollins Publishers and Reed Books.

Material from *By the Shores of Silver Lake,* text copyright 1939 by Laura Ingalls Wilder, renewed © 1967 by Roger L. MacBride. From *The Long Winter,* text copyright 1940 by Laura Ingalls Wilder, renewed © 1968 by Roger L. MacBride. From *Little Town on the Prairie,* text copyright 1941, copyright © renewed 1969 by Charles F. Lankin, Jr. From *These Happy Golden Years,* text copyright 1943 by Laura Ingalls Wilder, copyright renewed © 1971 by Roger L. MacBride. Reprinted by permission of HarperCollins Publishers.

Portions of Chapters 1 and 4 originally appeared in somewhat different form in my articles "The Symbolic Center: *Little House in the Big Woods,*" *Children's Literature in Education* 13 (1982): 107–14; "The Magic Circle of Laura Ingalls Wilder," *Children's Literature Association Quarterly* 10 (Winter 1985): 168–70; and "Laura Ingalls

Wilder's *Little House* Books: A Personal Story," in *Touchstones: Reflections on the Best in Children's Literature,* ed. Perry Nodelman, vol. 1 (West Lafayette, Ind.: Children's Literature Association, 1985), 291–300.

I am grateful to the following people for their help and encouragement: Carol Schumacher and Tess Larson, for reading the manuscript; Rita Conlin, Registrar of Deeds for Pepin County; Dwight M. Miller of the Herbert Hoover Presidential Library; and William T. Anderson.

Chronology

1867	Laura Elizabeth Ingalls born on 7 February near Pepin, Wisconsin.
1868	Ingalls family moves to Missouri.
1869	Ingalls family moves to Kansas (Indian Territory).
1871	Highly probable that Ingalls family moves back to Wisconsin.
1874	Ingalls family moves to Walnut Grove, Minnesota.
1876	Ingalls family moves to Burr Oak, Iowa.
1879	Ingalls family moves to De Smet, South Dakota.
1885	Laura Ingalls marries Almanzo Wilder on 25 August.
1886	Daughter, Rose, born on 9 December.
1890	Laura, Rose, and Almanzo move to Westville, Florida.
1892	Wilders return to De Smet, South Dakota.
1894	Wilders move to Mansfield, Missouri.
1911	First article, "Favors the Small Farm House," appears in *Missouri Ruralist,* 18 February.
1912–1923	Columnist and Home Editor for *Missouri Ruralist.*
1915	Laura visits her daughter Rose in San Francisco; writes poems for "Tuck 'Em in Corner" for San Francisco *Bulletin.*
1919	"The Farmer's Wife Says," *McCall's,* June.
1925	"My Ozark Kitchen," *Country Gentleman,* 17 January.
1932	*Little House in the Big Woods.*
1933	*Farmer Boy.*
1935	*Little House on the Prairie.*
1937	*On the Banks of Plum Creek.*

1938	*On the Banks of Plum Creek* named Newbery Honor Book.
1939	*By the Shores of Silver Lake.*
1940	*The Long Winter. By the Shores of Silver Lake* named Newbery Honor Book.
1941	*Little Town on the Prairie. The Long Winter* named Newbery Honor Book.
1942	*By the Shores of Silver Lake* given Pacific Northwest Library Young Reader's Choice Award. *Little Town on the Prairie* named Newbery Honor Book.
1943	*These Happy Golden Years.*
1944	*These Happy Golden Years* named Newbery Honor Book.
1949	Almanzo Wilder dies.
1953	*Little House* books reissued with new illustrations by Garth Williams.
1954	Laura Ingalls Wilder Award established; she is presented with the first award.
1957	Laura Ingalls Wilder dies on 10 February.
1962	*On the Way Home.*
1971	*The First Four Years. Little House* books issued in paperback.
1974	*West from Home.*
1988	*A Little House Sampler.*
1991	*Little House in the Ozarks.*

LITERARY AND HISTORICAL CONTEXT

1

Contexts: Current and Historical

In September 1974, NBC began the "Little House on the Prairie" series, which lasted nine seasons, won fifteen Emmies, and regularly ranked among the top twenty favorite shows until 1982.[1] This series brought worldwide fame to Wilder, and to the book that had given the series its title. Many readers have treasured Laura Ingalls Wilder's *Little House* books; but the television show, which at the time of this writing was being rerun on the Turner Broadcast System and in many other countries,[2] has reached many more people than the book, even though it has resulted in increased readership for anything written by Wilder.[3]

THE TELEVISION SHOW

The differences between the *Little House* books and the television show have troubled many readers.[4] For one thing, with the exception of the first episode, the setting is not Kansas but rather Walnut Grove, Minnesota. Second, the show is structured as if all eight books were about a little house on the prairie, and it uses many parts of the other seven books, often without being faithful to their order. Third, it adds many characters and incidents not found in any of the books. Fourth, the show clearly tries to appeal to viewers by inserting anachronistic episodes about contemporary problems such as drug abuse and discrimination against people with disabilities. Indeed, the show resembles the books only in its use of one of their titles, one of their settings, their main characters, and some events of the last five books (though not the setting: most of those events occurred in De Smet, South Dakota).

Actually, however, these differences between the books and the show are less disturbing than several more fundamental differences. The show is about a poor, loving, sustaining family living on a farm near a community central to the episodes. Aired during a time of public scandals and widespread disillusionment, this show—set in a past idealized by many Americans—was wholeheartedly patriotic. (Many people have compared it, with good reason, to "The Waltons," a show which ran during the same period [from 1972 to 1981] on CBS).[5] The two are obviously much alike. Unfortunately, the story told by the show, though it was what Americans wanted to hear during the 1970s, was not the story Wilder told in *Little House on the Prairie* or the other *Little House* books. *Little House on the Prairie* begins and ends with a journey, which comprises six of the twenty-six chapters. It is a novel about the frontier, about country inhabited by Native Americans;[6] Wilder thought of it as her "Indian story."[7] The Ingallses are frontier people more than they are pioneers, and pioneers more than farmers. In fact, try as hard as they might, the Ingallses are never really farmers, although Laura marries a farmer. In other words, the *Little House* books, and especially *Little House on the Prairie*, are about the wilderness more than a safe farm near an established community. They are about pioneering more than farming, about change and freedom more than stability or security, about family more than community. They are, of course, about both sides of each of these dichotomies and about the tension between them.[8]

The television show dissolves this tension to provide sentimental and often melodramatic nostalgia. It reduces the ambivalence, ambiguity, depth, and richness of the books to one side of the myth they embody—that of self-reliant Americans who through perseverance and hard work master nature sufficiently to allow their families to survive and to learn the values by which they live.

OTHER CONTEXTS

What became of *Little House on the Prairie* in the 1970s, when it was Ronald Reagan's favorite television show,[9] introduces only one of its many contexts and suggests the complexity of its meaning for the contemporary reader. Additional contexts to be reviewed are as follows: (1) the other *Little House* books; (2) American myth about the frontier and wilderness; (3) the Ingallses' experience in Indian Territory, the experience from which the novel arises; (4) Wilder' sources in writing *Little House on the Prairie* about 65 years after the Ingalls lived in Kansas (her memory, the memories of family and friends, and the research she did to verify and supplement these memories); (5) Wilder's historical position while she was writing the book in the depths of the Great Depression; and (6) our historical context as we read the novel in the late twentieth century. These various contexts will be explored in turn below.

But before I turn to an examination of specific contexts, a word about my purpose in doing so. The late twentieth century, often called the "postmodern" era, acknowledges the subjectivity of all knowledge and the consequent importance of understanding context as the source of interpretation and meaning.[10] Context shapes and limits us. Family, school, religion, government, society, and culture (especially as expressed in language), as well as biological inheritance and environment, form filters through which we view reality. Context determines what and how each of us perceives. To be sure, we can change our context, as it can change us. Locked in a hermeneutical circle or spiral,[11] we act out of our context, see the results, modify our actions, and thereby change our context. We then act out of this altered context and repeat the cycle. This is a much simplified account of the way we understand reality, for others in our context also affect and change our understanding and us. Simple as it is, however, this account of the interpretive circle by which we make meaning captures the essential interdependence of reality—any part is shaped by and shapes the other parts; no part is outside its context, and therefore no part is objective.

As we expand our context, we spiral in increasingly larger circles of interpretation. This, I believe, happens to any work of art admired by more than one generation, especially one that becomes by cultural consensus a classic.[12] Thus, *Little House on the Prairie* is shaped by and shapes about half a dozen contexts. I, of course, select these contexts and not others because of who I am. They are my context as I interpret the book. Other writers would select some or all of these contexts as well as others. Indeed, readers bring similar and different contexts which will lead them to agree with, question, or disagree with me. Given the current understanding of the nature of knowledge, I welcome the reader's involvement in interpreting the novel and look forward to a yet larger circle of understanding for *Little House on the Prairie*.

The Other Little House *Books*

Laura becomes a frontier girl in *Little House on the Prairie,* the third of the *Little House* books. *Little House in the Big Woods,* the first of the books, portrays her pioneer existence in relatively settled, safe Wisconsin.[13] *Farmer Boy,* the second of the books, shows us the abundance of food and hard work which are the experience of a successful farmer and his son—in this case, Laura's future father-in-law and husband on a farm in Malone, New York. Laura's father had purchased the Wisconsin land; Almanzo's father had purchased the New York land; but no one purchases the Kansas land in Indian Territory or the claim by Silver Lake. Laura's father ("Pa" throughout the books) homesteads.

The Homestead Act of 1862 lies behind the journeys and homes in *Little House on the Prairie, By the Shores of Silver Lake, The Long Winter, Little Town on the Prairie, These Happy Golden Years,* and *The First Four Years,*[14] although Pa actually files a claim only in South Dakota, outside of De Smet. The books seldom directly criticize the Homestead Act. One criticism does appear, however, in *These Happy Golden Years,* when a woman sitting on her family's claim explains:

> Whoever makes these laws ought to know that a man that's got
> enough money to farm, has got enough to buy a farm. If he hasn't
> the money, he's got to earn it, so why do they make a law that
> he's got to stay on a claim when he can't? All it means is, his wife
> and family have got to sit idle on it, seven months of the year. I
> could be earning something, dressmaking, to buy the tools and
> seeds, if somebody didn't have to sit on this claim. (119)

Getting enough income to farm and to stay in residence for a
specific number of months, however, as William Holtz points out, was
really only the first of many problems the homesteader faced. There
was no available land in the eastern woodlands. One had to homestead
on the prairie, where subsistence farming was impossible. There were
few, if any, suitable trees, so the homesteader had to depend on eastern markets for building materials and fuel. The east was also the
source of much food which could not be raised on the prairie because
of insufficient rainfall. Holtz contends, furthermore, that the homesteaders eventually learned that "more than 160 acres were needed to
sustain a family . . . [because] expensive new technology rendered the
farmer dependent on a cash crop, borrowed capital, vast transporta-
tion networks, and an international marketplace" ("Closing," 81).

On the Banks of Plum Creek, the fourth of the books, takes place
in Walnut Grove, Minnesota, where Pa trades his horses for land, bor-
rows money, and attempts farming, only to have his crop destroyed
for two years in a row by a plague of grasshoppers. This book comes
the closest of the eight (since *The First Four Years* was published
posthumously, I don't consider it part of the series) to reflecting the
difficulties of prairie farming as described by Holtz.

*By the Shores of Silver Lake, The Long Winter, Little Town on the
Prairie,* and *These Happy Golden Years* are all set in De Smet, South
Dakota, where blizzards and droughts take on enormous proportions.

The First Four Years covers the first years of Laura's and Almanzo's
marriage. In "Closing the Circle," Holtz criticizes *The First Four Years* in
terms of Wilder's failures as a realist in her prose and her vision. Here is
a dull, monotonous story of one disaster after another, resulting in Laura
and Almanzo Wilder's defeat by the prairie, very similar to the defeat of
the Ingallses near Walnut Grove. But this is a very different prairie from

that of five of the *Little House* books, especially *Little House on the Prairie.* Whereas Laura and Almanzo in *The First Four Years* farm during a major drought (1887 to 1894), there is sufficient water in the last four *Little House* books. In *Little House on the Prairie,* there are also sufficient trees for building a house and stable and for burning as fuel, and there is soil for growing vegetables and fruits. Most important, this novel takes the innocent, secure viewpoint of a child whose knowledge and understanding of the dangers in her life are limited and always mediated by her faith in her parents as experienced, responsible adults.

Home, farm, family, and good, abundant food are the focus of the first two books. But the land—the prairie—is the outstanding feature of the last six, especially of the third novel, as it was for everyone who homesteaded there. In *Where the Sky Began: Land of the Tallgrass Prairie,*[15] John Madson points out that "grassland of such magnitude was wholly alien to the western European mind" (xi). He suggests that "it diminished men's works and revealed them to a vast and critical sky, and forced people into new ways of looking at the land and changed them forever . . . , freeing them of certain dogma, breaking old institutions, and shaping new ones to fit the land" (xii).

The vastness of sky, land, and horizon hint of excesses of wind, flowers, sun, fire, and snow. The land also evokes thoughts of transcendence and God, as Madson indicates in his chapter "The Lawns of God." The prairie symbolizes freedom. At one extreme, it is terrifying to people who need the security of the known and the limited: Madson calls these "pioneers" (200). At the other extreme, it is exhilarating to those—Madson calls them "frontiersmen" (200)—who desire the risk of the unknown and the infinite. The prairie is wilderness, in contrast to the civilization left behind. Besides its excesses of sky, land, weather, and fire, it hides Native Americans and wolves. It teaches its inhabitants about openness and mindfulness, offering up "a thousand worlds within this one world of grass" (Madson, 27). Pa and Laura never tire of interacting with the prairie, while Ma and Mary prefer home and civilized ways.

In the course of the *Little House* books, Pa and Laura learn some of what Madson points out was needed for survival on the prairie: "a discarding of old tradition and methods, and a painful learning process in which men adapted to a new system of grassland existence" (203).[16] The thick sod, which often did not get moisture because of rapid evaporation and which required huge breaking plows and teams of oxen; life in a dugout made of sod; sod burned as fuel; fear of nearby Native Americans; "fever and ague"; fire; poor diet—all of these drove many people out and led those who survived to emphasize the tangible and the pragmatic. Their one ideal was freedom—from government, Native Americans, wolves, or any interference in their private affairs. They were fiercely independent and yet curiously dependent on and cooperative with one another (Madson, Part II: "The People"). The lazy and the shirkers were not tolerated. People had to be hardworking and responsible for themselves, but they willingly helped one another with any project that required more than one set of hands.

Beginning in *On the Banks of Plum Creek* and becoming the focus of the last two books, community is an important feature of the *Little House* books. Experiences of school and church occur in five chapters of the fourth book. In *Little Town on the Prairie,* only seven of the twenty-five chapters are not experiences of school, church, work in town, or other social activities. In *These Happy Golden Years,* as Laura becomes a schoolteacher and a married woman, she is not home for thirteen of the thirty-three chapters; and she is deeply involved in social activities throughout the book, as she and Almanzo court, become engaged, and marry. This novel's last chapter, "Little Gray Home in the West," echoing the title of the first *Little House* book—*Little House in the Big Woods*—ends the story of Laura's growing up, bringing it full circle, ready to begin the story of her daughter's growing up. William Holtz describes the series as follows: "The Little House books would preserve a version of her mother's life from childhood through marriage; it was essentially a frontier romance that delivered young lovers into a green and fecund world and stood, in its implicit values, as an archetypal American story" (*Ghost,* 350).

I would stress growing up more than the love story, which begins only at the very end of *Little Town on the Prairie* though it occupies much of *These Happy Golden Years.* To be sure, *Farmer Boy,* the second book, is about Almanzo's childhood, and he becomes a character in the series in *By the Shores of Silver Lake.* He also becomes the hero of *The Long Winter,* when he risks a journey on the blizzard-stricken prairie to buy the wheat the townspeople need to survive; indeed, some portions of this novel are told from his point of view. Still, Laura is clearly the hero of the series: seven of the books tell her story, mostly from her point of view, and her relationship with Almanzo primarily occupies only the last book.

Myth

In the pioneers' attitude toward the prairie and all its natural inhabitants and phenomena, as described by Madson, we find the ambivalence, ambiguity, richness, and depth of American myth—a contradictory myth that powered the spiritual, social, political, and physical development of this country.[17]

On the one hand, there are the pioneers as God's tools, confronting the frontier and converting the wilderness to civilization, a concept expressed most notably as the doctrine of "manifest destiny." This myth has allowed Americans to stress individualism to the point of enslavement of other races or even genocide. It has fostered an emphasis on the pragmatic and the tangible, especially technology and exploitation of the land by means of this technology—with little thought for the future. Americans' wandering spirit, our inability to commit ourselves, our denial of limits and tragedy, our faith in technology and progress, our acting as if there will always be an abundance of resources, and our belief that hard work and perseverance will bring economic and social success—these are all to a large extent results of this myth of the pioneer on the frontier.

On the other hand, there is the wilderness as the garden of Eden, giving the pioneer access to God. Madson notes this aspect as well, especially in his chapter "The Lawns of God." Behind this myth is a desire for innocence, oneness, and transcendence. Uncivilized, the wilderness symbolizes nature before the fall. Nash points out that from the beginning, Americans saw the wilderness as making them different from the old world (67) and as making them the "medium through which God spoke most clearly" (69). The Transcendentalists, especially Emerson and Thoreau, saw nature as symbolic of the spirit, and civilization as the destroyer of humanity (Nash, chap. 5). Their spirit reappeared in the preservationist John Muir, whose favorite metaphor for "wilderness" was "the book of God" (Nash, 124).

Nash's thesis is that we have two concepts of wilderness. We define it as chaos, disorder, darkness, confusion—as uncontrollable, demonic space. But we also see it as a source of vigor, strength, goodness, life, inspiration, creativity, spiritual connection, and renewal—as sacred space. When there was little civilization, the negative image of wilderness dominated. As civilization grew, the positive image became more prominent, especially in nineteenth-century romanticism throughout European-American civilization—just as American pioneers were settling the wilderness. Typically, pioneers were not as romantic about the wilderness as were people in civilized areas. Today, of course, with very little wilderness left, its positive image dominates.

Wilder wrote the *Little House* books between 1930 and 1943, fully aware that there was no more frontier to conquer, no more west to settle, and little opportunity for children to experience wilderness. In her Book Fair speech in Detroit in the fall of 1937, she said:

> I began to think what a wonderful childhood I had. How I had seen the whole frontier, the woods, the Indian country of the great plains, the frontier towns, the building of the railroads in wild, unsettled country, homesteaders and farmers coming to take possession. I realized that I had seen and lived it all—all the successive phases of the frontier, first the frontiersman, then the pioneer, then the farmers, and the towns. Then I understood that in my own life I represented a whole period of American History. That the frontier was gone and agricultural settlements had taken its place when I married a farmer. It seemed to me that my childhood had been much richer and more interesting than that of children today.[18]

"Indian Territory"

In 1869 the Ingalls family traveled from Missouri to Kansas.[19] They homesteaded, according to the 1870 census, "in the eighty-ninth residence in Rutland Township" in the "SW 1/4 Sec. 36," Montgomery County.[20] A replica of the little house on the prairie can be visited northwest of Tyro, Kansas (on Highway 166), and about 13 miles southwest of Independence, Kansas (on Highway 75), about 20 miles from where I grew up in Coffeyville, Kansas. Walnut Creek lies about one-quarter of a mile north, and the Verdigris River about 10 miles to the east. There were Osage camps northeast and southeast of this homesite,[21] both near the Verdigris River; Native American trails are still evident nearby (Thurman, 9).

In 1803, when it passed to the United States as part of the Louisiana Purchase, all of Kansas was Indian Territory. Its first inhabitants were Kansa, Osage, Wichita, Pawnee, and Pueblo. Kansas became a state in 1861, but much of it remained Native American reservations,[22] and the Cherokee Strip (2.5 to 3 miles wide and 276 miles along what is now the southern border of Kansas) was not part of the state. As early as 1854–55, treaties and laws began to provide for the removal of Native Americans from these reservations (Zornow, 92–105), but those in what is now southeastern Kansas—the Osage and the Cherokee—were the last to give up their land. The Diminished Reserve of the Osage lay just north of the Cherokee Strip and was 50 miles wide and 100 miles long. On 15 July 1870, Congress made provision for the sale of the Osage land in Kansas;[23] in September 1870 the Osage agreed to move; and beginning in June 1871, settlers were able to buy land vacated by the Osage (Zornow, 103). The Cherokee Strip became part of the state after the Cherokee agreed to sell it as one provision of a treaty with the federal government signed in July 1866, but the land did not become available to settlers until the summer of 1872.[24] By then there were few Native Americans left in southeastern Kansas.

The Osage, whom the Ingallses watch depart in the fall of 1870, returned from their winter hunt to their new reservation in Oklahoma. They had once lived between the Gulf of Mexico and the Missouri River and between the Mississippi River and the Rocky Mountains, roaming and hunting as they wished. They were tall people, and the men wore their hair, as Wilder describes it, shaved on the sides with the top hair pulled up and wrapped so that it stood up. Having lost much land to whites through treaties, they struggled to hold onto this last bit in Kansas, although it was difficult for them to find buffalo, and settlers continued to crowd them. The Cheyenne, Sioux, and Arapaho wanted them to make war, but the Osage refused. Perhaps some of them did steal from the pioneers; they were hungry and angry that once again their treaty with the government was turning out to be only lies. Pa—like all the other settlers—knew he was homesteading on Native American land (*LHP*, 47). Because claims began to be filed in June of 1871 and Pa did not file one, we might assume that the Ingallses left before then.

Not much more is known about the history behind *Little House on the Prairie*. The beautiful hand-dug well is still on the property. Carrie was born in August 1870, while the Ingallses lived in Kansas. There is a gravesite in Independence for Dr. George A. Tann, who was black and a homeopathic surgeon for the Osage (Thurman, 10). There were other neighbors, mostly not mentioned in the book—William H. Scott, a farmer; James L. Scott, a surveyor; Joseph James; Alexander Johnson; John Rowles; Ed Mason; Robert Gilmore; John Friendly; a Mr. Riddle; and their families (Zochert, 34–35). The coming of the railroad after the Civil War opened up the range, and cattle drives from Texas and Oklahoma became common, resulting in one of Kansas's major industries.

Wilder's Sources

Laura, who had been born on 7 February 1867, was only one year old when the Ingallses left Wisconsin. Pa sold the little house in April 1868 and moved the family to his parents' house until they were ready to begin their long journey with Uncle Henry and Aunt Polly to Missouri. They lived in Missouri until fall 1869, when Uncle Henry's family returned to Wisconsin and Laura's family left for Kansas.[25]

Obviously, Wilder relied on Pa's, Ma's, and Mary's memories for the events of *Little House on the Prairie,* or rather—since they died in 1902, 1924, and 1928, respectively—on her memories of what they had told her. She did write something about her life and mail it to her mother and her sister sometime before 1915.[26] After her mother's death, she also wrote to her mother's sister, Martha Quiner Carpenter.[27] In addition, we know that she wrote to the Oklahoma and Kansas historical societies to inquire about the name of the Osage leader she calls Soldat du Chêne and received a letter from an R. B. Selridge of Muskogee, Oklahoma, confirming that "the Chief of the Osages at that time was named Le-Soldat-du-Chene."[28] Zochert claims

Laura Ingalls Wilder, 1927.

that Wilder and her daughter, the writer Rose Wilder Lane, drove to Oklahoma, seeking the site of the little house on the prairie. This may be true; certainly Garth Williams thought the little house on the prairie was in Oklahoma, perhaps because Oklahoma was Indian Territory in the 1860s and 1870s. Wilder probably did not know about the Osage Diminished Reserve or the Cherokee Strip in Kansas, although she or Lane may have read some of the books Grant Foreman listed for them.

Wilder remembered some of the trip back to Wisconsin, which probably happened in 1871. Her first draft of the *Little House* books, which she called "Pioneer Girl,"[29] places the near-disaster fording the stream on the way out of Kansas and the fire in the chimney in a little house in Missouri where they stayed for a brief while on the way home to Wisconsin. More important, "Pioneer Girl" begins almost immediately with the events of *Little House on the Prairie,* because in her life this journey occurred before the events in *Little House in the Big Woods.* It seems probable, however, that Laura didn't clearly remember why they returned to Wisconsin. The Osage had signed a treaty and moved to their reservation before the Ingallses left. There were threats that settlers would be removed, but these must have ceased once the treaty was signed. Had the Ingallses lived in the Cherokee Strip, they might still have been threatened, but it seems clear that they lived just inside the southern border of the Osage Diminished Reserve. Zochert suggests that Pa decided to return after he received a letter from the man farming the Wisconsin land, saying that he was going west and returning the land to Pa (46). If this is the case, Pa's decision seems contradictory (if Wisconsin was too crowded when they left, it must still be so) and even less flattering than his not wanting to wait until the soldiers put him out. It suggests a wanderlust.

Why do we care? Knowing that Wilder had no memory of these events, we can quit thinking of them as factual autobiography and begin to evaluate them as autobiographical fiction—that is, in terms of Wilder's artistic choices. One of these choices, obviously, was to begin with the snug, secure little house in the big woods, in which food was always plentiful, and turn to adventure next, in the second book about Laura, when readers were already familiar with Pa's and Ma's ability as providers and protectors.

Wilder's Location in History: The Great Depression

Little House on the Prairie appeared at the depth of the Great Depression in 1935.[30] From the beginning, the publishing fate of the *Little House* books was affected by the times. Knopf, which had originally accepted *Little House in the Big Woods,* closed its juvenile division before the novel could be published. Knopf handed it on to Harper, which published it enthusiastically but then rejected the first draft of *Farmer Boy.* One of the reasons Harper gave for refusing this draft of *Farmer Boy* was unwillingness, during the Depression, to gamble on a book which did not seem as strong as *Little House in the Big Woods.* For the draft that was eventually accepted, Harper offered only half the usual royalty, citing financial constraints due to the Depression.[31] Rose Wilder Lane stayed on her parents' farm from 1930 to 1935, to a large extent because of finances. There she was able to help her mother with her writing, to watch what was happening to the country as the Depression deepened, to discuss politics with her mother, gradually to abandon all her liberalism, and increasingly to infiltrate the *Little House* books with her growing conservatism.

Both Lane and her mother disapproved of Franklin Delano Roosevelt's socialist liberalism. They seemed to have little understanding of, and no sympathy for, the suffering and poverty of many Americans. In addition to the financial collapse begun with the fall of the stock market on 21 October 1929, farmers on the plains were enduring the worst drought this country has ever experienced (Parrish, 252–303). Large numbers of urban workers, who had left farms to work in the booming factories of the 1920s, were now laid off. John Kenneth Galbraith provides some telling statistics: the average number of workers unemployed every year between 1930 and 1940, except for 1937, was 8 million, or one in four (168). People all across the country were starving, and volunteerism failed. Charities and local relief activities provided insufficient assistance (Parrish, 251). Michael Parrish claims that the Great Depression resulted largely from "laissez-faire, unrestricted competition, and survival of the fittest" (244) in business and resulted in human misery for workers. Galbraith, John Garraty, and Robert McElvaine all agree.

Roosevelt was elected because he promised jobs and security. In a series of steps, some of which were found unconstitutional, he established limits on big business and provided relief for the poor. The Agricultural Adjustment Act, Banking Act, Federal Power Commission, Public Utilities Holding Company Act, WPA, National Labor Relations Act, Wealth Tax Act, Federal Writers' Project, and Federal Artists' Act—and social security—"changed the face of America for the next half century" (Parrish, 340). Roosevelt put people to work and shifted the power structure so as to give more power to the working and middle classes. Perhaps his greatest contribution was to end what Galbraith calls the "sense of utter hopelessness" (187) that dominated the country during the early 1930s.

The house in Mansfield: Rocky Ridge Farm.

Wilder and Lane had been relatively untouched by the Depression. They did lose some investment income, but Lane did not tell her mother about this until after the first *Little House* book had been published (*Ghost*, 226–29). And they always had the farm. This perhaps explains why they stood back in horror at the decidedly different course that Roosevelt was steering for the United States. Lane in particular was extreme. Her writing during the remainder of her life was increasingly polemical nonfiction. She became obsessed with the errors of a government that turned away from the principle of the self-reliant, responsible individual and toward a practice of increasing taxes so that government could provide for the weak (*Ghost*, 256–87).

Lane's stand is abundantly clear in the following passage from her *Old Home Town,* published in 1934:

> Now some of us seem to see, in our country's most recent experience, an unexpected proof that our parents knew what they were talking about. We suspect that, after all, man's life in this hostile

universe is not easy and cannot be made so; that facts are seldom pleasant and must be faced; that the only freedom is to be found with the slavery of self-discipline; that everything must be paid for and that putting off the day of reckoning only increases the inexorable bill. This may be an old-fashioned, middle-class, small-town point of view. All that can be said of it is that it created America. (23–24)

In the *Little House* books, this philosophy is expressed directly, as many critics have noted,[32] in *Little Town on the Prairie,* when Laura realizes:

Americans won't obey any king on earth. Americans are free. That means they have to obey their own consciences. No king bosses Pa; he has to boss himself. Why . . . when I'm a little older, Pa and Ma will stop telling me what to do, and there isn't anyone else who has a right to give me orders. I will have to make myself be good. (76)

In his review of popular movies and novels of the 1930s, McElvaine argues that "the myths of the past become the agenda for the future" (220). As I have already suggested, I believe that the *Little House* books were successful during the Depression because of the highly ambiguous American myth they embody. Lane's message about freedom and responsibility is part of this myth, and it is the part that the television series emphasized. But in tension with this dominant theme in the *Little House* books are the themes of "faith in the future, . . . persistence, hard work, beneficence and occasional destructiveness of nature, the centrality of family, [and] the search for community" (Miller, 35). McElvaine identifies the American myth as "two opposing sets of values. . . . Both are individualistic; but one emphasizes cooperation, the other competition" (201). In his opinion, the "Depression bred sharing—community, justice and cooperation" (207). People realized that by sticking together, they could resist oppression. He calls this "cooperative individualism" and opposes it to "competitive individualism," which characterized the "amoral individualism and the marketplace" of the 1920s (221). To the contemporary eye, both kinds of individualism pervade the *Little House* books. But for the Depression-era reader, the books would all have highlighted the importance of cooperation in the struggle for survival; ordinary people are valued for their ethical behavior. Then as now, though, the books could also be read nostalgically, as portraits of a simpler, better time.

The Contemporary Reader

In the late twentieth century, the educated reader brings all of these contexts and perhaps others to a reading of *Little House on the Prairie*. Children, the book's intended audience, will, of course, not bring as many contexts. They will, however, bring their culture, imbibed through their daily living, and some part of that culture will be the American myth. Toys, television, family, school, books, malls, religion—all will in varying degrees have formed children's sense of how to live and what to desire or despise. In children, we can see clearly reflected what our society values.

What do we see? Various forms of oppression are evident even among first-graders—sexism, racism, ageism, ableism, classism, heterosexism, colonialism, and consumerism. They have learned the lesson of power in our society—that who we are at birth determines how much power we will have. The white, European male with control over others—control that usually comes with money, possessions, and position—will have the most power. The "others" controlled by him will include animals, vegetables, minerals, and other creatures and features of the earth besides humans. Control may require conquest and may involve abuse. For the sake of achieving power, violence may be employed.

In *Habits of the Heart: Individualism and Commitment in American Life*, Robert Bellah and his colleagues explore the ramifications of our society's concept of individualism as something that can exist apart from relationship.[33] They point out that we can know ourselves only when we are engaged in relationships and that the consequences of denying this reality are a loss of community and ultimately a loss of self. To the extent that individuals exploit anyone else for their own ends, therefore, they isolate and lose themselves. Unfortunately, the consumerism dominant in American society encourages individualism and the exploitation of others. Many Americans continue to live or to believe that they should live by what is actually only half of the American myth. We too often forget or don't know that cooperation, or mutuality, has always been a part of this myth. Mutuality is increasingly needed as an ethic for our times. Characterized by respect, equity, and reasonable limits, it seeks to empower all those involved. In the case of relationships with nature, the word "sustainability" is simply a variant of the word "mutuality." Here, too, the goal is the maximum good of everyone and everything involved.

"Habits of the heart," in other words, control our every behavior. If we believe that individualism is the good to be sought and that others are simply a means to this end, we ignore our dependence on others. In the late twentieth century, awareness of the interdependence of all life is at the forefront. We fear for the life of the earth and turn our attention to ecology. Careless of the ozone layer, rain forests, and certain species necessary to a biosphere—and with a mania for driving cars, for consuming, and for wasting—we destroy the earth and ourselves, mostly ourselves. We are rapidly making the earth uninhabitable for humans. Here is our most dramatic lesson about relationships. "Mutuality," "sustainability," "cooperation," or "balance"—whatever word we use, we are learning as the century closes that our very lives depend on our ability to form just relationships with all that exists.

This is, in other words, a question not of "either-or," but of "both-and." Opposition between individual and community or individual and nature is false. To have one, we must have the other, and so every individual deserves justice as a part of the web of existence on which our very lives depend. To some degree, awareness of our interdependence is part of the filter through which the contemporary reader views the American myth as expressed by *Little House on the Prairie.* Even more than during the Depression, or at any time before our own, what McElvaine calls "cooperative individualism" and I would call "interdependence" or "mutuality" is necessary for our survival as a species.

THE STRUCTURE OF THIS STUDY

What are the "habits of the heart" in *Little House on the Prairie?* What does it offer us on the verge of the twenty-first century? Does its version of the American myth provide some wisdom for our time?

In the next six chapters, I address these questions. In Chapter 2, "The Critics' Journey," I give an overview of the critical reception of the novel since its publication. This is essentially a journey from initial concern with the book's reflection of Wilder's life and American history to contemporary concern with its implications about race, gender, and other oppressive concepts. In Chapter 3, "The Outer Journey: How to Be a Pioneer," I examine the novel's attention to detail, for what it suggests about who the pioneers were and in preparation for Chapter 4. In Chapter 4, "The Circular Journey: The Structure of the Novel," I discuss the symbols built by careful attention to detail and patterns—the circle, the line, and chaos. In Chapter 5, "The Mythic Journey: How to Live," I examine the cosmological, mystical, and pedagogical implications of these patterns, that is, their religious meaning, especially in relation to the other seven *Little House* books. Chapter 6, "The Inner Journey: Laura's Development," examines Laura's psychological growth in *Little House on the Prairie,* as well as in the other seven books. Chapter 7, "The Historical Journey: American Myth," places this novel and the series as a whole in the context of our national mythology and explores the ways in which it does and does not reflect that mythology.

Finally, the Appendix, "Approaches to Teaching *Little House on the Prairie,*" suggests ways to teach students to read the novel so that they can perceive its attention to detail, its structure, its mythic dimensions, and Laura's psychological development.

2

The Critics' Journey

Most North Americans and many people in the rest of the world know and admire *Little House on the Prairie,* many having read the book as a result of their fondness for the television show. Today there are more than 20 million copies of the *Little House* books in circulation, and translations into 40 languages.[1] Over 40 million copies have been sold. Both *Little House on the Prairie* and *Little House in the Big Woods* are among the ten "all-time bestselling children's books" in paperback (fourth and seventh, respectively).[2] The eight *Little House* books have been popular since their publication during the 1930s and the early 1940s (the years of the Great Depression and the beginning of World War II). Five of the *Little House* books are Newbery Honor books (though *Little House on the Prairie* is not one of them). As a major contribution to children's literature, the set of eight *Little House* books received the Laura Ingalls Wilder Award—named after her and given to her in 1954. *Little House on the Prairie* is Wilder's most famous book, undoubtedly because of the success of the television show.

The critical reception[3] of *Little House on the Prairie* when it was first published did not indicate the status that it would eventually acquire. It was reviewed positively, but the Newbery Committee passed it by; the committee recognized children's love of this book only after the popularity of the series had become evident with publication of *On the Banks of Plum Creek* in 1937. But since 1953, when the books were reissued with Garth Williams's illustration and received a glowing review by Anne Carroll Moore in *Horn Book Magazine,* the series as a whole has widely been accepted as classical children's literature, and the number of critical works about the series has steadily increased.

An overview of this criticism reveals that critics have primarily been interested in this novel in terms of its creation; its use of some specific character (for example, the wolf) or activity (such as teaching or music); its use of language and patterns to create powerful, moving symbols; its reflection of the frontier and myths about the frontier; its implications about gender and race; its evidence that Wilder changed structure and literary techniques as the books were intended for increasingly older children; and its authorship as mother-daughter collaboration.

CREATION

The earliest criticism explored how the series had been written, published, and illustrated. Pieces by Garth Williams and Virginia Kirkus included in the special issue of *Horn Book Magazine* in December 1953 are examples. So is Donald Zochert's biography, evolving out of a central concern to show differences between Wilder's life and the series. Indeed, this was the principal critical concern until the 1970s; it resulted in our coming to understand the extent to which Wilder pruned and shaped her memories, creating fiction rather than autobiography.

A recent work concerned with this side of Wilder's writing is the historian John Miller's *Laura Ingalls Wilder's Little Town: Where History and Literature Meet.* Miller uses the historical record—newspapers and documents, for example—and concludes that the novels are remarkably true to history. That is, the details of the novels do not contradict historical fact. On the other hand, he suggests a wealth of detail that Wilder did not use. Here again a critic comments on Wilder's artistic choices as determined by her vigilant attention to her presumed readers—children.

A SINGLE CHARACTER OR ACTIVITY

Four studies exemplify this type of critical response, Arthur Arnold's "Big Bad Wolf"; Catherine Gates's "Image, Imagination, and Initiation: Teaching as a Rite of Passage in the Novels of L. M. Montgomery and Laura Ingalls Wilder"; Muriel Whitaker's "Perceiving Prairie Landscape: The Young Person's View of a Western Frontier"; and Jan Susina's "Voices of the Prairie: The Use of Music in Laura Ingalls Wilder's *Little House on the Prairie.*"

Three of these studies are essentially comparative. Arnold examines stereotypical and incorrect portraits of the wolf in many works of children's literature, including Wilder's novels; he also chastises Wilder for stereotyping Native Americans. Gates also limits her focus to a specific feature of the series: in this case, Laura's attitude toward and experience of teaching. Gates finds Laura similar to Anne Shirley in L. M. Montgomery's books, in that for both girls, teaching is a rite of passage to adulthood. Whitaker surveys many novels all set on the prairie but evoking differing attitudes about it. She puts Wilder's *Little House on the Prairie* among those that portray the prairie as an earthly paradise. She also identifies this understanding of the prairie as the myth most common in children's literature.

Susina also focuses on only one feature of *The Little House on the Prairie:* its use of music. His purpose, though, is to enrich our understanding of this one novel. His careful analysis of auditory imagery—imagery of sounds created by humans and by nature—reveals how the language and structure of this novel create powerful, evocative symbols. Like Gates, Susina finds an earthly paradise where people live in harmony with nature. Another study may also be mentioned in this regard: the chapter on folklore in Janet Spaeth's *Laura Ingalls Wilder*. Spaeth explores the novel's use of folklore much as Susina explores its music.

SYMBOLISM

Five studies in addition to Susina's find that the book's creation of powerful symbols accounts for much of its appeal: Rosenblum, "Intimate Immensity"; Bosmajian's "Vastness and Contraction of Space"; my own "Magic Circle" and "Symbolic Center"; and Frey's "Laura and Pa: Family and Landscape." Like Susina, all four of these critics see the prairie as a symbol.

Rosenblum describes the prairie as mythic space portrayed with "intimate immensity." Bosmajian builds on Rosenblum's work, pointing out that the expansion and contraction of this space results in readers' experiencing the prairie as either a paradise or a hell, depending on whether or not the space seems intimate. For example, when everyone is at home on a moonlit summer night and the birds sing with the fiddle, mythic space is paradise; but when the Ingallses are confined to the house and Native Americans' war cries fill the prairie, mythic space is hell.

My articles on Wilder's use of the circle and its center expand on both Rosenblum and Bosmajian. I find that, in the individual novels and in the series as a whole, Wilder uses the circle not only as a symbol but also as a structural device. Typically, she ends where she began—in winter, on the prairie in search of a home, in a little house. I classify the novels as close to myth primarily because of their careful construction of images from many evocative details and their placement of each image to compare and contrast with others so that a pattern of meaning (a myth) emerges.

Frey examines Wilder's use of Laura's viewpoint, showing how, as is typical of a young child, Laura exhibits great imagination and tends to fuse with her father and with the prairie to experience the bliss of being without clear boundaries. Thus, Frey too focuses on the portrayal of the prairie as an earthly paradise.

THE FRONTIER AND MYTH

Several critics have placed this work in the context of American attitudes toward the frontier—as a fact of American history and as a myth about who Americans are. An early study by William Jacobs, "Frontier Faith Revisited," began the exploration of what the novel means to us in terms of its treatment of the frontier, focusing on its frontier values: for example, self-reliance and responsible neighborliness. Roger Barker's more recent exploration of the same subject—"The Influence of Frontier Environments on Behavior"—details both the positive and the negative effects of the frontier on moral values. Barker points out that the frontier encouraged lawlessness and in turn vigilantism. People became judge, jury, and executioner of those who threatened their communities, and this was not without ill effects on those "on the side of justice."

Fred Erisman's studies of Wilder's series all concern his perception of these books as regionalism—that is, literature set in specific areas of the United States and mostly defined by recreating a sense of what it was like to be there. In this case, of course, the historical period is the settling of the American frontier.

William Holtz's "Closing the Circle" enriches the commentary about Wilder and the frontier. Holtz shows how physical conditions in the places where the Ingallses tried to homestead ensured failure for most of those who came from areas requiring a very different kind of farming. He notes the mythic nature of Wilder's books: they never recognize or identify realistic reasons why Pa fails to "strike it rich."

Finally, an additional study is Janet Spaeth's chapter on pioneering in *Laura Ingalls Wilder*.

GENDER AND RACE

A large number of critical studies deal with Wilder's descriptions of gender arrangements and race relations. Elizabeth Segel's "Laura Ingalls Wilder's America: An Unflinching Assessment" was first. It was followed by Anna Thompson Lee's "'It Is Better Farther On': Laura Ingalls Wilder and the Pioneer Spirit"; Sarah Gilead's "Emigrant Selves: Narrative Strategies in Three Women's Autobiographies"; Janet Spaeth's chapter on Wilder's feminism; Louise Mowder's "Domestication of Desire: Gender, Language, and Landscape in the

Little House Books"; and Anne Romines's "Preempting the Patriarch: The Problem of Pa's Stories in *Little House in the Big Woods*." Clearly, this is a central critical concern, especially with regard to *Little House on the Prairie,* where Native Americans are more of a presence than in any of the other books and where Laura is more often outside with Pa than inside with Ma (as she is in the first book and in the last two).

What is interesting about this criticism, as I will discuss in detail later,[4] is its ambivalence about Wilder's portrayal of Laura and of Native Americans. It raises questions which I feel have yet to be resolved and which this present study makes one more attempt at resolving.

Is Wilder sexist or not? Is Pa a typical patriarchal pioneer, clearing away the wilderness to make way for progress? Or does Wilder moderate her portrait, making him an American hero (like Huck Finn, Ishmael in *Moby-Dick,* or Nick Adams in Hemingway's short stories) who experiences nature as sacred? Should Laura identify with him in his irresponsible urge to take his family farther and farther west? Or should she identify with Ma, who is the family's anchor throughout the series. Is Ma stereotypical? Are female or male values in charge of the novel?

Similar questions are raised about the Native Americans. Is Wilder racist or not? Who in the novel seems racist? Ma? Pa? Laura? How clear are the attitudes of each of these characters? Don't Pa and the Native Americans have a lot in common? Doesn't Laura wish to be like them?

Whatever we may conclude about Wilder's sexism and racism, or her freedom from sexism or racism, her characterizations are obviously not simplistic.

FORM AND THE INTENDED READER OF THE *LITTLE HOUSE* BOOKS

Three critics have explored how Wilder's books change as they are intended for increasingly older children. In my own articles, I describe the books as moving from mythic romances, where the focus is on *place* as ideal or demonic and on its transformation of Laura, the heroine; to adventure story in *On the Banks of Plum Creek* and *By the Shores of Silver Lake;* to psychological and social realism in the last three books. In one chapter of her *Laura Ingalls Wilder,* Janet Spaeth looks at ways in which language and content in the different books reflect Wilder's own growing up. Recently, Margaret Mackey (in "Growing with Laura") has also seen how this series, consciously intended for progressively older readers, reveals differences between books for younger children and books for older children. Mackey examines different treatments of time and space throughout the series. This area, where we have barely scratched the surface, presents a rich field for critical development.

MOTHER-DAUGHTER COLLABORATION

Scholars now recognize that Rose Wilder Lane, Laura Ingalls Wilder's daughter, played a major part in the creation of the *Little House* books.[5] Five critics have written about the mother's and daughter's roles in this process: William T. Anderson, Anita Claire Fellman, Caroline Fraser, William Holtz, and Rosa Ann Moore. Currently, the degree to which Lane "wrote" the *Little House* books is the primary critical concern.

Moore was the first to discover the collaboration between Wilder and Lane. Her first study was a comparison of *The First Four Years* and *These Happy Golden Years* in terms of events common to both. She held that five characteristics of the latter make it superior to the former: (1) there is a poetic and philosophic dimension; (2) events are dramatized; (3) the material is appropriate and appealing to children; (4) characterization is consistent and vivid; and (5) a sense of form controls the work, relating each part to other parts, creating a whole, and relying on a consistent point of view ("Laura Ingalls Wilder's Orange Notebooks," 110). In the rest of this article, Moore details how the orange notebooks, or rough draft, of *These Happy Golden Years* are similar to *The First Four Years* in terms of these five characteristics, concluding that Wilder was a skilled editor.

Rose Wilder Lane, about 1930.

By the time she wrote her second article, Moore knew that the skilled editor had been Lane, as Donald Zochert, Wilder's biographer, had suggested to her ("Rose-Colored Classics," 14). Moore had catalogued the Lane and Wilder papers in the possession of Roger Lea MacBride, heir and executor of Lane's estate. She saw in Lane's revisions of Wilder's early magazine work and in the correspondence between mother and daughter, particularly in their correspondence about *By the Shores of Silver Lake,* sufficient evidence of Lane's editing. She concluded, however, "We see Laura holding her ground against Rose about theme, characterization, and fact, while Rose wins the battles on plot and style. Further, the evidence of Rose's own fiction demonstrates the improbability of her having been able to create the Little House books on her own" (14).

Moore's third article is a careful examination of 19 letters written by Wilder and Lane about *By the Shores of Silver Lake*. By this time, Moore was ready to say that "Wilder's artistic mastery over the techniques of writing were very uncertain . . . [and her] naive recollection was insufficient to create and sustain the dynamic group of novels which we have today" ("Chemistry of Collaboration," 101). Here she credits Lane with the necessary "objectivity" and "craft" and Wilder with the "life and perspective" and concludes that "the real chemistry of the collaboration escapes definition and lies somewhere in the realm of psychological reality which never got onto the paper and remains forever beyond our grasp" (103).

Anderson was the next to probe the nature of the collaboration, carefully detailing Wilder's "literary apprenticeship" to Lane from 1919, when she edited a piece her mother wrote for *McCall's* about marrying a farmer, to 1932, when Harper published *Little House in the Big Woods*. In addition to the correspondence, Anderson studied Lane's diaries, which were finally available in 1980–81 in the Herbert Hoover Library of West Branch, Iowa ("Literary Apprenticeship," 290). These made it obvious that Lane had revised "Pioneer Girl," Wilder's initial story of her life (a first-person account, beginning with her early childhood in Indian Territory and ending with her marriage), but—having failed to interest a publisher—carved out a picture book. When a publisher expressed interest in something like it but longer, Lane spent almost three weeks revising and rewriting her mother's first draft of *Little House in the Big Woods*.

A second article by Anderson reveals that Lane also played an extensive role in the creation of the book about her father's childhood, *Farmer Boy*—perhaps an even greater role than for *Little House in the Big Woods*. After the first manuscript was rejected by the publisher, Lane visited the farm in Malone where her father had grown up, and then (over about two months) did a second revision of the *Farmer Boy* manuscript, which was published in 1933. Anderson's contention is that Wilder was a storyteller who learned from her daughter the craft of transforming her material into writing, a process which he believes was largely complete by the time Wilder began *Little House on the Prairie.* "In the process of writing her third juvenile, she would begin to incorporate the methods of characterization and dialogue that Lane had been patiently trying to teach her, leaving less for Rose Wilder Lane to do and taking a stronger hand in the crafting of her own books" ("Continuing Collaboration," 143).

Fellman and Holtz give more credit to Lane than either Moore or Anderson does, but both focus primarily on Lane's political views as they are increasingly expressed in the *Little House* books. Fellman argues that Lane's unhealthy relationship with her mother while working on these books taught her to be a "hard right" conservative, emphasizing the presumably American virtues of self-reliance, ingenuity, emotional stoicism, freedom, and responsibility—and therefore little governmental control over the individual. Similarly, Holtz says that "at least since *Little House on the Prairie,* Rose had been heightening the ideological potency of her mother's stories by emphasizing the primacy of the individual and the meddling role of the government" (*Ghost,* 306).

Caroline Fraser, in a more recent article in *The New York Review of Books,* lamented that "it is now widely and unjustly assumed that Laura Ingalls Wilder is not the true author of her books" (44). I agree. Like Fraser, I have carefully read the handwritten manuscripts of *Little House on the Prairie* and "found extensive corrections and revisions in Wilder's own hand" (Fraser, 44). No typescript of the novel is available, but comparing the handwritten manuscripts with the published book certainly proves that Lane was the editor—not the author—of Wilder's books. As Fraser points out:

> Lane seems to have simplified, clarified, and modernized her mother's old-fashioned and sometimes clumsy diction, spelling, and grammar. She also seems to have added transitions to the beginning of the books and to some of their chapters. She may also have revised passages, adding or expanding dialogue, and changed the order of some chapters for dramatic effect. But this is not certain, since we can never know much about the communi-

cation between Wilder and Lane while the two women were living next door to each other for the first five years that Wilder was
working on her series. (44)

Fraser goes on to note that Lane's diaries and the correspondence between mother and daughter reveal Lane's close reading of the
books, their quarreling over different aspects of the books, and their
"discussions of technique and revisions . . . via the telephone or over
the teacups at the Rocky Ridge Farm" (45). Like Moore, Fraser sees
Lane's own fiction as our best proof that Wilder is the principal writer
of the *Little House* books.[6] She rejects Holtz's description of Wilder's
prose as "pedestrian" and describes Lane's writing as sentimental and
conventional.[7] Again, I agree completely, as I do with her conclusion
that "in the collaboration of writer and editor, Wilder and Lane, they
combined their strengths and minimized their weaknesses. But it is also
clear that, of the two, Wilder was the genuine writer" (45).

A READING

3

The Outer Journey: How to Be a Pioneer

In *Little House on the Prairie,* Wilder celebrates the details of pioneer life. Her attention to detail, in fact, characterizes the book. For each activity of building a home and living as a pioneer, she records a step-by-step process. She also describes characters and settings in great detail. Because she does all this, a way of life unfamiliar to her readers becomes available: they can vicariously experience pioneering in "Indian Territory" during the 1860s and 1870s. As Caroline Fraser notes, "The particularity with which each of the most humble of human undertakings is described . . . is fascinating in and of itself, a vivid record of a lost way of life" (41).

The narrator's careful attention to persons, places, things, and activities serves additional functions as well. In Hamida Bosmajian's words, "Laura Ingalls Wilder's style always anchors the child-reader's and Laura's egos in reassuring specificity."[1] As we will see, Laura's attention to the physical features and activities of her life gives her and the reader a sense of security before, during, and after each experience of danger. "The attention to detail is . . . an emotional refuge, . . . [capturing] a child's ability to ease anxiety by losing herself in the contemplation of the orderly and ordinary" (Fraser, 41).

Most important, in this novel *attending* is a value—perhaps the highest value. It demonstrates caring or loving. It is the value that Robert

Bellah and colleagues identify as essential to "the good society." In their conclusion to *The Good Society*[2]—"Democracy Means Paying Attention"—and throughout that book, they explore what it means to pay attention at all levels of life: from the family to the environment; political economy; government, law, and politics; education (technical and moral); the public church; and America in the world. As they explain it:

> Attention is, interestingly enough, a religious idea in more than one tradition. Zen Buddhism, for example, enjoins a state of mindfulness, an open attention to whatever is at hand; but Zen practitioners know this is always threatened by distraction. Mindfulness is valued because it is a full waking up from the darkness of illusion and a full recognition of reality as it is. (255)

Bellah and his colleagues note that mindfulness, "common enough in Eastern religions" (255), is also present in Hebrew and Christian scriptures, and they assert that self-control and self-discipline are essential to genuine attentiveness and can be learned only from others—in the first place from family. They conclude that the ability to pay attention arises from and expresses the "basic trust" acquired in a child's earliest experience with his or her parents.[3] To the extent that children learn to trust their parents, they learn to see "reality, Being itself," as "trustworthy" (*Good Society,* 284), attend to it carefully, and become "ambassadors of trust in a fearful world" (286).

I believe that Wilder is such an ambassador. She carefully attends to places, animals, persons, things, and activities on a continuum ranging from the civilized to the wild, and she reveals that such attention to the world and life is itself transforming.

PLACES

Prairie
Little House on the Prairie displays Wilder's love of "the inhuman ways of the world" (Fraser, 38), especially her love for the prairie. The book is full of the sights, sounds, smells, and feel of the prairie. The prairie

prevails in the first four chapters, and only gradually is it rivaled by the little house. Even after Pa begins to build the house in Chapter 5, attention to the prairie still generally opens and closes each chapter, serving as the background. Occasionally the prairie again becomes the foreground—for example, in Chapter 14, "Indian Camp." And the last two chapters return to the prairie, as once again the Ingallses leave a little house and make a covered wagon their home.

Our view of the prairie is through Laura's eyes, and it changes from the beginning to the end of the book. At first Laura isn't quite sure what she feels about the prairie. She knows Pa wants to go there because "the land was level, and there were no trees. The grass grew thick and high. There the wild animals wandered and fed as though they were in a pasture that stretched much farther than a man could see, and there were no settlers. Only Indians lived there" (*LHP*, 2). But as they travel across the prairie, Laura feels mostly boredom:

> Kansas was an endless flat land covered with tall grass blowing in the wind. Day after day they traveled in Kansas, and saw nothing but the rippling grass and the enormous sky. In a perfect circle the sky curved down to the level land, and the wagon was in the circle's exact middle.
>
> All day long Pet and Patty went forward, trotting and walking and trotting again, but they couldn't get out of the middle of the circle. When the sun went down, the circle was still around them and the edge of the sky was pink. Then slowly the land became black. The wind made a lonely sound in the grass. The camp fire was small and lost in so much space. But large stars hung from the sky, glittering so near that Laura felt she could almost touch them.
>
> Next day the land was the same, the sky the same, the circle did not change. Laura and Mary were tired of them all. There was nothing new to do and nothing new to look at. (13–14)

In Chapter 4, "Prairie Day," Laura begins to get acquainted with the prairie, with its meadow larks, "small pearly clouds," dickcissels, "grasses blowing in waves of light and shadow across it" (40), rabbits, prairie chickens, "little, brown-striped gophers" (43), hawks, phoebes, and mockingbirds. What she finds makes her happy:

The wind sang a low, rustling song in the grass. Grasshoppers' rasping quivered up from all the immense prairie. A buzzing came faintly from all the trees in the creek bottoms. But all these sounds made a great, warm, happy silence. Laura had never seen a place she liked so much as this one. (48–49)

Pa's experience is also positive. He comes home saying that the country's full of game—deer, antelope, squirrels, rabbits, birds of all kinds, and a creek full of fish. He says, "There's everything we want here. We can live like kings" (50).

This happy first impression deepens into a love affair as Laura experiences the prairie during every kind of weather and each season of the year from one spring until the next, in her father's absence and presence, and with Native Americans nearby or far away. For the reader, the prairie serves as the barometer of her emotions.

Her favorite seasons are spring and summer. One of the novel's most lyrical passages celebrates the coming of spring when "after the Indians had gone, a great peace settled on the prairie. And one morning the whole land was green" (312). The suddenness of the greening, the return of the birds, the busyness of the small animals and the Ingallses during the day, the singing of the birds at nightfall, and the family's resting and singing in the starlight—these are Laura's experience of spring and summer. The ovenlike heat and stillness of midsummer (172–74); the brown, gold, and red and the fierce wind ("norther") of autumn (199–226); and the dull grasses, wailing wind, cold rain, spitting snow, thick-coated animals, short gray days, and dark cold nights of winter (232, 238, 253, and 255)—these, along with the birds and animals, are the substance of her songs to the prairie seasons.

However, Laura's sense of safety or danger determines her view of the prairie. When she is afraid, she cannot see the details, but only the huge, empty, silent prairie. As Bosmajian explains, referring to Gaston Bachelard's work,[4] vastness will threaten the fragile ego with loss of self (Bosmajian, 54–56). Dependent on her father for her very existence on the prairie, Laura prefers to stay in the house when he is gone. "Outdoors was too large and empty to play in when Pa was away" (208). Even with Pa, as they walk out into the prairie in

Chapter 14 ("Indian Camp"), "Laura felt smaller and smaller. Even Pa did not seem as big as he really was" (174).

Similarly, after more and more Native Americans begin turning up everywhere, and grow louder each night than the night before (286–88), "Laura . . . had a queer feeling about the prairie. It didn't feel safe. It seemed to be hiding something. Sometimes Laura had a feeling that something was watching her, something was creeping up behind her. She turned around quickly, and nothing was there" (288). On the other hand, the Native Americans' departure from the prairie, like Pa's absence, leaves nothing "but silence and emptiness. All the world seemed very quiet and lonely" (311).

Although the prairie sometimes threatens her, she comes to love it, as Pa does, for the sense of freedom it brings. Pa insists that he would have this sense of freedom even if the prairie were settled.

> Laura knew what he meant. She liked this place, too. She liked the enormous sky and the winds, and the land that you couldn't see to the end of. Everything was so fresh and clean and big and splendid. (75)

As Bosmajian points out, if vastness does not threaten the ego, it can create a consciousness of the sublime, "an oceanic feeling in which the ego loses its boundaries" (62) and becomes one with the world. We see Laura as capable of such trust (largely in her father) at the end of the novel. "They were all there together, safe and comfortable for the night, under the wide, starlit sky. Once more the covered wagon was home" (335). Pa sings by the firelight, and "she felt her eyelids closing. She began to drift over endless waves of prairie grass, and Pa's voice went with her singing: . . . 'Row your boat lightly, love, over the sea; / Daily and nightly I'll wander with thee'" (335).

The House

The other major place in the novel is the house. The story begins when the Ingallses leave one house; "they drove away and left it lonely and empty in the clearing among the big trees, and they never saw it again" (1). The story ends after they leave another little house to sit "lonely in the stillness" (325). In between Wilder celebrates home building—

walls (Chapter 5), moving in (Chapter 6), doors (Chapter 8), fireplace (Chapter 9), roof and floor (Chapter 10), well (Chapter 12), furniture (Chapters 12 and 15), and all the things they have brought west for their home—Ma's china shepherdess, red-checked tablecloth, spider, bake-oven, dishes, and pans; Pa's violin, gun, and tools.

Interruptions in the construction of the house threaten the Ingallses and reinforce their need for it, even while revealing its inability to keep them safe from wolves (Chapter 7), fever 'n' ague (Chapter 15), panthers (Chapter 20), fire (Chapters 16 and 22), and, especially, Native Americans (Chapters 11, 18, 21, and 23). Indeed, when the Ingallses are forced to stay inside in fear of Native Americans, the little house threatens Laura as much as the huge prairie does whenever she experiences it as "absence." "Both, extreme constriction and all-filling vastness, suck in or swallow the fragile ego" (Bosmajian, 52).

But often the little house is a home—providing comfort and safety. As Laura tells us:

> The house was pleasant. The good roast chicken was juicy in Laura's mouth. Her hands and face were washed, her hair was combed, her napkin was tied around her neck. She sat up straight on the round end of log and used her knife and fork nicely, as Ma had taught her. She did not say anything, because children must not speak at table until they are spoken to, but she looked at Pa and Ma and Mary and at Baby Carrie in Ma's lap, and she felt contented. It was nice to be living in a house again. (119)

When Pa finishes the floor, Ma says, "Now we're living like civilized folks again" (129), identifying the house as a symbol of civilization in contrast to the wild prairie.

As Pa completes the house, Laura's love for the prairie increases. In Chapter 10, after the construction of walls, doors, and fireplace, we find Mary and Laura at play in the prairie—hunting birds' nests and watching flocks of prairie chickens, striped snakes, and great gray rabbits. Only after the well is dug and the cow tamed do they venture any distance from the house, going with Pa to the Native American camp. That Laura likes the prairie better and better as the house is built suggests that the safety of the house allows her to seek out the mysteries of the prairie.

"Living like civilized folks again."

But this little house "on the prairie" is never as safe as the house "in the big woods." The big woods sheltered and concealed the first little house. The prairie is merely a surface, frequently described like an ocean—for example, in the passage and picture in which Pa puts the wagon cover on the house as a roof, and also in the last scene of the book. On this surface, the little house rests, exposed and visible to the weather, wild animals, fire, and Native Americans.

Other Places

Although the little house and the prairie are the principal settings, there is a continuum of places ranging from the town to the flood-swelled creek that once nearly carries away the wagon and later nearly prevents the girls from having gifts at Christmas.

A roof—or a sail—for the little house on the prairie.

In this book, water and fire are the wild elements that threaten Laura. Fire is the most intense threat. The fire in the chimney that could have burned the house down and killed Mary and Carrie, had Laura not courageously pulled them out of the way, is a forerunner of the much more terrible prairie fire that Pa and Ma successfully fight off with a backfire. But water is also a significant threat. Frozen Pepin Lake could have cracked and swallowed up the Ingallses and their covered wagon; later, the flood-swollen creek nearly overcomes the Ingallses and their wagon and does carry Jack the bulldog away. The water rises suddenly in the well Pa has dug and might have drowned him. All these are examples of water as a wild element. This wildness, like that of the Native Americans, threatens the Ingallses with loss of control and even loss of life. For Ma and Mary, furthermore, it opposes civilization.

At the other extreme is the "town." There are two towns in the novel, Pepin and Independence. As a source of supplies, both are necessary to the Ingallses, but Pa's trips alone to Independence are frightening to the family left behind. His returns, on the other hand, celebrate the comforts and delights of the things he has bought in town. Thus the town opposes wildness.

For Pa, nevertheless, town is too crowded. At the beginning of the novel, Wilder tells us that Pa leaves Wisconsin because "wild animals would not stay in a country where there were so many people" (2). By the end of the novel, we see that Laura has learned to share Pa's preference for "country where the wild animals lived without being afraid" (2).

The Native Americans also live here without being afraid. They live in the hollows of the prairie, like the one Pa, Mary, and Laura explore in "Indian Camp." They live not in houses but in tents, cooking over campfires, wearing leather moccasins and clothes or going without them, leaving bones around on the ground, and keeping their ponies nearby. This wilderness is clearly their home.

Finally, there are the creek bottoms where wild animals live:

> Here grew the tall trees whose tops Laura had seen from the prairie above. Shady groves were scattered on the rolling meadows and in the groves deer were lying down, hardly to be seen among the shadows. The deer turned their heads toward the wagon, and curious fawns stood up to see more clearly. (18)

All the wild animals come to drink from the creek, including the great buffalo wolves and clouds of mosquitoes, carrying malaria. Here the Ingallses pick blackberries, chop down trees to build the house, and collect rocks to build a fireplace and chimney.

ANIMALS

Animals are either domesticated and associated with the house, or wild and of the prairie. The continuum ranges from Jack, the brindle bulldog, who—very much a member of the family—lives in the house, to the panther whose scream wakes the Ingallses and sends Pa out into the "black dark" (256) of the prairie. In between are Pet and Patty, the mustang ponies, and Pet's offspring, Bunny; the cow that must be tamed before she can be milked; her calf; the cattle the cowboys drive to market; the Indian ponies that are ridden without bridles or saddles; all the birds, frogs, snakes, rabbits, squirrels, prairie chickens, and other small creatures of the prairie; and the wolves that encircle Pa and Patty, and then encircle the little house one moonlit night. These wolves keep Pa and Jack alert inside the house—which still has no doors—but Pa holds Laura up to the window to observe their beauty.

In Wilder's attention to animals, we again see "her love for the inhuman world" (Fraser, 38). Laura tells us more about Jack than she does about Mary. She laments his loss after he disappears as they cross the swollen creek. She trusts him, along with Pa, to keep her safe. When he must be chained to keep him from attacking Native Americans, she repeatedly tries to comfort him. Similarly, Laura describes how Pet and Patty look and what they do. The cow, the cattle, and the Indian ponies receive less attention, but this seems to be simply because they enter the novel toward its end and are a focus only in two chapters, "Texas Longhorns" and "Indians Ride Away."

A good part of Wilder's description of the prairie is lyrical attention to its small inhabitants. It is impossible not to feel her joy in, for example, a meadowlark's flight, a nightingale's or mockingbird's song, or the sounds of frog and goose.

"The Wolf-Pack" and "A Scream in the Night" are about wild animals—wolves and a panther. The panther, perhaps because Laura never actually sees it, seems even wilder than the wolves. Then, too, Pa emphasizes how dangerous the panther is, telling Laura that it would carry off a little girl, "and kill her and eat her, too" (261). An especially frightening aspect of the episode with the panther is the darkness of this night, unlike the moonlit night when the wolves encircle the house.

In light of more recent understanding of the wolf as a highly intelligent animal, unlikely to attack humans, Arthur Arnold accuses Wilder of "tolerance rather than understanding"[5] of the wolves. In fact, he also accuses Wilder of racism, finding similarities between the wolves' and the Native Americans' threats to the house. Although we may see some truth in his evaluation, there is evidence that Wilder not only feared wolves (and Native Americans), but also admired and even envied them. Her description of the wolves conveys awe rather than tolerance. Pa is amazed that the wolves surround him and Patty, "trotting along, and jumping and playing and snapping at each other, just like dogs" (90). That night his and Laura's behavior is reverential. The moon, the nearness of the wolves, their size, the sound of their breathing, the beauty of the leader's gray coat and green eyes, their encircling the house, and their howling at the moon—all of these are ingredients of magic.

PEOPLE

The previous paragraphs suggest that in this novel *place* receives more attention and carries greater weight than characterization. Indeed, people are characterized largely in terms of their association with places. Ma and Mary belong in the house, as does Mrs. Scott. Laura and Pa love the prairie. Mr. Scott seems less comfortable than Pa with the prairie; Mr. Edwards and Dr. Tan, a bit more so; the cowboys even more so; and the Native Americans are completely at home. Tension between house and prairie conveys that either may represent good or evil.

Mrs. Scott

Mrs. Scott, for example, is one voice of civilization, and from our historical distance she might be judged evil. For her, "the only good Indian was a dead Indian" (211). A spokeswoman for manifest destiny, she explains that the Native Americans "never do anything with this country. All they do is roam around over it like wild animals. Treaties or no treaties, the land belongs to folks that'll farm it. That's only common sense and justice" (211). Mrs. Scott represents one extreme.

Ma

Ma, whom Laura clearly understands as the standard by which one measures morality, does not like Native Americans, but she never voices sentiments like Mrs. Scott's. Nevertheless, she is clearly racist when she deplores Laura's yelling and tanned skin as "Indian"-like (122). Similarly, she refuses to wash her clothes in the creek as "Indian women do" (76) and associates washing clothes in a tub, having a wood floor, and having a fireplace with being "civilized" (129). Afraid of Native Americans, she perceives them as inferior to white folks because they look different and live differently.

If prejudiced, though, she is also gentle, quiet, and steadfast. Determined to teach Mary and Laura their proper gender role, she reveals the strength and force of the pioneer woman as the civilizer of the frontier.[6] She is one of the many images of the frontier woman who, as a sturdy helpmeet for her husband, was known as "the Madonna of the Prairies, the Brave Pioneer Mother, [or] the Gentle Tamer."[7]

Mary and Carrie

Like Ma, Mary is good. Unlike the sometimes naughty daughter, Laura, she never interrupts, never speaks unless spoken to, never talks with her mouth full, never runs and yells like an "Indian," and always keeps her sunbonnet on and tied. Beyond this, we know very little about Mary. As the "good little girl," she, like baby Carrie, is a type. Laura's sisters function as her foils. Mary contrasts with Laura, who does all of what Mary never does and little of what Mary always does. Laura often displays what Ma considers faults in a lady—that is, "impulsiveness, restlessness, and a wayward temper" (Lee, 80). Carrie also contrasts with Laura, who frequently is determined not to cry or be greedy like a baby.

Laura

We share Laura's viewpoint and experience her as the most interesting and complex of the characters. We forgive her faults, recognizing that she is still a young child. Indeed, as contemporary readers, we delight in her "feminist" resistance to Ma's insistence that she behave like a lady. We are pleased to have her admire and imitate her father, Mr. Edwards, and the cowboys, even as we recognize that her faults are also her father's (Lee, 80). We may suspect what we can discover in later books—that she will grow up to be the equal of her husband on the farm.[8] Pa seems larger than life to Laura. She trusts him to keep her safe. She sees the prairie as he does. The space activates her imagination, as it does his. Curious, open, energetic, fully alive to the moment, she is her father's child—tagging along as he builds the house, listening

with wide eyes to his stories, and experiencing his music as enchant-
ment, bringing the stars within his reach (37) and setting them to dancing (66) and singing (51).

Pa promises Laura that she will see a papoose when she gets to
"Indian" country, and her questions about the papoose are a refrain
throughout the first ten chapters of the book, repeatedly reminding us
of the Native Americans' presence until we actually encounter the two
"Indians in the House" (132–46). Perhaps because of Pa, Laura does
not fully share Ma's attitude toward Native Americans. She is afraid of
them but also curious about them, feelings that color our view of them.
She reports that they wear little clothing, only fresh skunk skins which
smell terrible; that their red-brown bodies are thin; that their faces are
"bold and fierce and terrible" (139); that they have only a tuft of hair
on the top of their head (which is how the Osage wore their hair); and
that having eaten what Ma cooks for them, they leave.

Later, with Pa, she will admire the Osage chief Soldat du Chêne,
who also comes to the house, shares dinner and smokes a pipe with
Pa, and later convinces other Native Americans—perhaps the
Cheyenne, Sioux, and Arapaho—not to make war with the white
folks. As Pa says, refuting Mrs. Scott's opinion, "That's one good
Indian!" (301). When the Native Americans leave the area permanently, in a long line led by this chief, Laura grieves inarticulately. She
is fascinated by their ponies, which are free of saddle and bridle; and
by their children, who are free of clothes, "all their skin . . . out in the
fresh air and sunshine. . . . She had a naughty wish to be a little Indian
girl" (307). When she finally sees a papoose and looks into its eyes, all
she can say is, "'I want it! I want it!'" (308). When asked why, "'Its
eyes are so black,' Laura sobbed. She could not say what she meant"
(309), and she could not stop crying.

Many have interpreted this chapter of *Little House on the Prairie*
as an elegy for the Native American way of life and have seen Laura as
identifying with and as sympathetic to the Native Americans—for
example, Bosmajian (57), Segel (69), Spaeth (75–76), and Mowder
(17). Bosmajian and Mowder also interpret Laura's "I want it" as indi-
cating that she has already imbibed the pioneer's urge to own and control the wilderness. Certainly, Laura's story in *Little House on the*

Prairie can be read as a quest for a papoose, who finally appears only to disappear forever, ending any possibility of relationship. It is also possible to understand "I want it," in which the papoose has no gender, as an effort to express her desire for all that she intuits about the Native American way of life.

The metaphors here are the papoose and, even more specifically, the papoose's black eyes—"eyes black as a night when no stars shine" (308). As an image of wilderness, they are provocative, suggesting mystery, the unknown, and that which is beyond human control. That Laura is not frightened of blackness is surprising, as is her response to Dr. Tan, the African-American homeopathic doctor for the Osage who cares for the Ingallses when they come down with malaria. "Laura had never seen a black man before and she could not take her eyes off Dr. Tan. He was so very black. She would have been afraid if she had not liked him so much" (191). In western thinking, blackness, darkness, and wilderness have functioned as metaphors for evil. Here we see those metaphors turned on end.

Laura's response to the departure of the Native Americans can be explained partly by her personality: she is her father's daughter, and she loves the wilderness. But her response goes beyond what she has learned about Native Americans from either parent. She has questioned her parents. Her mother's dislike has perplexed her and led her to ask why they came to "Indian country" (47) if Ma does not like them. Ma responds that "she didn't know whether this was Indian country or not. She didn't know where the Kansas line was. But whether or no, the Indians would not be here long. Pa had word from a man in Washington that the Indian Territory would be open to settlement soon" (47).

Laura's efforts to understand Native Americans and the Ingallses' relationship with them and their land emerge fully after Ma sings of Alfarata, a "wild . . . Indian maid" (235):

> Laura asked, "Where did the voice of Alfarata go, Ma?"
> "Goodness!" Ma said. "Aren't you asleep yet?"
> "I'm going to sleep," Laura said. "But please tell me where the voice of Alfarata went?"

"Oh I suppose she went west," Ma answered. "That's what Indians do."

"Why do they do that, Ma?" Laura asked. "Why do they go west?"

"They have to," Ma said.

"Why do they have to?"

"The government makes them, Laura," said Pa. "Now go to sleep."

He played his fiddle for a while. Then Laura asked, "Please, Pa, can I ask just one more question?"

"May I," said Ma.

Laura began again. "Pa, please may I—"

"What is it?" Pa asked. It was not polite for little girls to interrupt, but of course Pa could do it.

"Will the government make these Indians go west?"

"Yes," Pa said. "When white settlers come into a country, the Indians have to move on. The government is going to move these Indians farther west, any time now. That's why we're here, Laura. White people are going to settle all this country, and we get the best land because we get here first and take our pick. Now do you understand?"

"Yes, Pa," Laura said. "But, Pa, I thought this was Indian Territory. Won't it make the Indians mad to have to—"

"No more questions, Laura," Pa said, firmly. "Go to sleep." (236–37)

Her courageous questions clearly foreshadow her response in "Indians Ride Away."

Laura doesn't understand Ma's racist view of Native Americans and, resisting Ma's efforts to make her genteel, follows the impulses of her own heart and imagination. As I have already shown, Laura needs and loves the little house, but neither more nor less than she needs and loves wilderness. She is both her mother's and her father's daughter— a balance of the two. This becomes increasingly obvious as we move through the series; Laura learns to appreciate the security, variety, and community of civilization and the patience, steadiness, cheerfulness, inventiveness, and generosity of her mother's efforts to meet her family's need for survival and their desire for occasional luxuries. Indeed, in Wilder's attention to detail we see her mother's understanding that things are precious in and of themselves and absolutely necessary for human survival and dignity. We see her creating the intimacy that Ma made of every house Pa bought or built.

Pa

My discussion of Laura suggests that, on this continuum, Pa is more identified with wilderness than Laura is. But this is not wholly true. Pa's relationship with wilderness is more complex and ambiguous than Laura's. His every act destroys what he loves, "assuring the end of the age-old harmony of man and animal with the natural world" (Segel, 70). In his gender role, as prescribed by western civilization, he must provide for his family by building a house, shooting animals for them to eat, plowing up the prairie, and agitating for the removal of the Native Americans to land farther west. On the other hand, at the end of *Little House in the Big Woods,* we see him forgetting his need to shoot a deer for his family and experiencing oneness with a doe and her fawn in the moonlight. And at the beginning and all the way through *Little House on the Prairie,* he expresses his love for wild animals and wilderness. He also expresses his admiration for Native Americans, especially for Soldat du Chêne.

He will not side with the doctrine of manifest destiny as voiced by Mrs. Scott, or with the Scotts' opinion that "the only good Indian is a dead Indian." After the prairie fire, when Scott and Edwards think the Native Americans set it to burn out the settlers, Pa offers the following opinion:

> He figured that Indians would be as peaceable as anybody else if they were let alone. On the other hand, they had been moved west so many times that naturally they hated white folks. But an Indian ought to have sense enough to know when he was licked. With soldiers at Fort Gibson and Fort Dodge, he didn't believe these Indians would make any trouble. (284–85)

Obviously, Pa has a blind spot. He wants to live peacefully with Native Americans and doesn't want to disturb the wilderness. He doesn't see that his very presence makes his desire an impossibility. Pa is a dreamer. Playing his fiddle, he sits in the doorway, neither of the house nor of the prairie, whereas Laura is of both. Restless, striving for what he will never have, he builds a house carefully and is ready to abandon it as soon as the wilderness is gone. He does this in Wisconsin and then in Kansas. His reason for leaving the little house on the prairie does not seem convincing. Everything we know about him suggests that with this home finished and the Native Americans gone, he would not want to stay. Like the Native Americans, he is by nature a wanderer; but unlike them, he significantly alters the landscape to make the kind of home with which his family is familiar and comfortable. Although Laura will learn eventually that her freedom must be internal, Pa seeks a *place* where he can be free. Lee calls his "a wish for the forever unattainable, and to some extent, a wish to escape reality and adult responsibility" and points out that although Wilder never saw—or at least never acknowledged—Pa's failures as a provider, the evidence is there in the later books (84).

Other Characters

I have already pointed out that Mr. and Mrs. Scott share the same opinions about Native Americans. Mr. Edwards feels the same. Mr. Edwards, however, because he is a bachelor, seems even more of a wild man than Pa; in fact, he calls himself a "wildcat from Tennessee" (63). The wandering cowboys singing to their steers are even wilder than Pa and Mr. Edwards, who are at least momentarily stationary. The Native Americans, in Laura's eyes, are the "wild men" (56) and the children are even wilder than their parents. The papoose, with its black eyes, is her symbol for wilderness.

THINGS

Food

Food plays a major role. Laura often describes the Ingallses' meals and sometimes even recipes and methods of cooking. For example, there are corn cakes of cornmeal, salt, and water cooked in the bake-oven;

coffee; and salt pork fried in the spider for dinner on the trail (30). Bacon, coffee, and pancakes are eaten for breakfast (39). Cold corn cakes spread with molasses are a lunch (46). Juicy roast chicken is their supper the first night in the house (119). The turkey dinner at Christmas includes sweet potatoes baked in the ashes and wiped clean, salt-rising bread, stewed dried blackberries, and little cakes (254). We know that Pa shoots rabbits, prairie chickens, ducks, turkey, and deer for meat; that white sugar and flour, pickles, and crackers are rarities, usually reserved for company; and that a cow to provide milk and perhaps butter is a remarkable gift.

Household Goods

Household goods are also carefully listed and described in the last chapter, "Going Out": bedding made into two beds, the small cupboard full of dishes—tin plates, cups, and knives and forks—two carpetbags full of their clothing, Pa's rifle, straps, bullet pouch, and powder horn, his fiddle in its box, the black iron spider, the bake-oven, the coffeepot, the tub, the water bucket, the horse bucket. We hear elsewhere of Pa's hammer, ax, and wedge and of Ma's china shepherdess and red-checked tablecloth.

We know that the girls and Ma wear long-sleeved dresses with full skirts that button up the back and sunbonnets; that Pa wears a long-sleeved shirt, trousers with a belt, and tall boots; that the girls often go barefoot; that they wear nightgowns and nightcaps to bed; and that they have rag dolls.

Of the furniture, the Ingallses carry only the cupboard into Kansas and take only it and a willow rocking chair out. Furniture is not essential because Pa can always make new. Bedsteads, tables, stumps for chairs—these are all left behind in Kansas.

Special Possessions

Bosmajian points out that the three main characters possess things that set them apart from one another and illuminate their respective personalities (57–60). Laura has the word "papoose"; Pa has his fiddle; Ma has her china figurine. Like the furniture, and unlike food and household goods, these things are not necessary for physical survival.

But without these things, it would be impossible to know any of these characters as we come to know them.

Laura, the child who will become the writer, plays with a word that evokes reverie about where they are going, what will happen, why it happens, and what it means. Her questions about the Native Americans reveal a mind at play with the concept of wild people. At least once we hear this reverie directly: "Pa knew all about wild animals, so he must know about wild men, too. Laura thought he would show her a papoose some day, just as he had shown her fawns, and little bears, and wolves" (56). Like wild animals and the prairie, Native Americans are not real to her, as she reveals when she cries out for the papoose. But she does have provocative words and images, with which her imagination builds a vision of wilderness—a vision constructed of desire and yearning for a better life, free of unnecessary rules of behavior and dress and welcoming to Native Americans.

Pa's fiddle is much like Laura's word, expressive of his yearning, vivid, and often inarticulate imagination. Laura believes that Pa's playing moves and expresses the natural world. As he can inspire stars and the whole night to dance and sing along, he can answer the nightingale in its own language. Thus his fiddle transforms the world, as does Laura's word.

Similarly, Ma's china shepherdess transforms the cabin, making it a genteel, civilized space where women are imagined as fragile and delicate and the world and nature as idyllic or Edenic. Frivolous, an unnecessary possession, like Laura's word and Pa's fiddle, it too expresses a dream and a yearning imagination—in this case, yearning for a civilization in relation to a natural world properly tamed.

All three things speak of the necessity for imagination, vision, and hope. The same I believe is true of Chapter 19, "Mr. Edwards Meets Santa Claus." The delicious and civilized story Edwards concocts about meeting Santa Claus in Independence; the children's amazement that each of them receives a tin cup, a strip of candy, a heart-shaped cake covered in white sugar, and a new penny; and the splendid dinner—all this appeals to and expresses a human need for the special, for reality enlarged, elevated, and colored by the yearning imagination. The brightly colored beads that Mary and Laura find in the "Indian Camp" and the headbands with cutout stars that Pa brings from Independence serve the same function.

ACTIONS

My focus on concrete details and vivid images may have left a mistaken impression that this book is entirely description. Quite the contrary: this is a book of action. We learn about a campfire as one is built—from a space cleared of grass to kindling, logs, and coals. We learn about meals as they are shot or harvested, put together, cooked, and eaten. We learn about the house as it is built from walls to door, roof, floor, fireplace, and well. We learn about the prairie as it is watched, played on, hunted in, and crossed. Mindfulness is the essence of Wilder's style, but as Thich Nhat Hanh emphasizes in *The Miracle of Mindfulness: A Manual on Meditation,* to be mindful is not merely to sit and meditate. "The miracle is to walk on earth . . . keeping one's consciousness alive to the present moment."[9] To live mindfully is to be both anchored in the moment and open to its possibilities. Such is the genius of the author and her characters in *Little House on the Prairie.*

4

The Circular Journey: The Structure of the Novel

LITTLE HOUSE ON THE PRAIRIE AND LITTLE HOUSE IN THE BIG WOODS

Structurally, *Little House on the Prairie* is much like *Little House in the Big Woods*. Many of my observations in "The Symbolic Center," my article about the first *Little House* book, are therefore also true of *Little House on the Prairie*, the second *Little House* book about Laura (though the third to be published).

There are a number of parallels between the two books: (1) Each is more a vision than a plot centered on a conflict. (2) Each exhibits tension in style and structure. (3) Each balances polarities that threaten to conflict. (4) In each, Wilder's style relies heavily on antitheses, that is, on contrasting words, phrases, and clauses in parallel constructions. (5) In addition to antithesis and balance, Wilder uses repetition to give structure to gradual accumulations of details about places, animals, people, things, and actions. (6) In each, the key to style and structure is antithetical balance—in diction, images, sentences, and chapters. (7) This stylistic and structural device results in evocative symbolism. (8) Each novel has a circular pattern—highlighted by one cycle of the seasons—of descent and ascent, a movement from an idyllic world to a demonic world, and back again. (9) As Northrop Frye explains in *The Secular Scripture,*[1] this is the pattern of romance, which (in contrast to realistic fiction) is antirepresentational and obviously designed, contrasting characters, settings, and events to embody the extremes of wish fulfillment and nightmare.

But *Little House on the Prairie* also contrasts sharply with *Little House in the Big Woods.* As I have pointed out in "The Magic Circle of Laura Ingalls Wilder,"[2] *Little House in the Big Woods* emphasizes the center; *Little House on the Prairie* emphasizes the circle. At the beginning and end of *Little House on the Prairie,* the center is, paradoxically, a moving covered wagon, focusing our attention on the wild, endless prairie. Once their home stops moving and becomes a camp and then a little house, there are still no trees or other obstructions to their view of this prairie. The house, as we have already noticed, seems less protected, solid, and stable than the one in the big woods. At first, it is a skeleton house open to the light, air, and danger. Roofed with the canvas cover of the wagon, it seems more a boat than a house, not only in Garth Williams's illustration but also in Wilder's imagery. The little house is not "*in* the big woods" but "*on* the prairie," as a boat is not in but on the ocean.

As Dolores Rosenblum points out in "'Intimate Immensity': Mythic Space in the Works of Laura Ingalls Wilder," *Little House on the Prairie* is no less visionary than *Little House in the Big Woods.*[3] But it focuses on big rather than little, on universe rather than home, on wildness rather than domesticity. It holds oppositions in tension so that we experience what Gaston Bachelard calls "intimate immensity" (*The Poetics of Space,* chap. 8)—whereas in *Little House in the Big Woods* we experience immense intimacy. The first *Little House* book nurtures Laura and the reader, engendering the bliss of security within; then *Little House on the Prairie* releases them into the universe, evoking the bliss of freedom without.

VISION

This book's image of freedom, the Kansas prairie, is the most power-ful of Wilder's many magic circles. Bachelard points out in the last three chapters of *The Poetics of Space* that as an archetype, the circle can evoke experiences of movement or stasis, freedom or security, the sublime or the intimate, constriction or release. As a finite form, it confines and keeps safe or, if too small, traps. As an infinite form, it frees us into the timeless or eternal realm of dreams or nightmares.

In *Little House on the Prairie*, the circle of grass pulled up from around the wagon each night prevents the possibility of prairie fire, the buffalo wolves circling the skeleton house never attempt to get in, and the circle of backfire around the house protects it from prairie fire. The prairie on a sunny day after the house is built lulls Laura into bliss-ful reverie. On the stormy days before Christmas, though, it confines her in the house, anxious that Santa Claus won't find them. When Pa is nearby, the wide-open prairie is her delight; but when he is absent, she feels uneasy outside and often retreats to the house. Finally, when the war cries of the Native Americans surround the house, it provides neither intimacy nor safety, even though Pa is inside with her. Clearly, the prairie is wild, and Laura and her family are in danger as they never were in the big woods. But repeatedly the magic circle keeps them safe.

The prairie, furthermore, contents Pa because "no matter how thick and close the neighbors get, this country'll never feel crowded" (74). More important, here Laura encounters the wilderness that she had only heard about in the first novel. She sees the beauty of the wolf and wants to be a Native American child. Her experience leads her to share Pa's love for the wild free spaces of this earth. Inarticulate as she is, we see the seeds of this love when the Native Americans leave the territory and Laura shames herself because she cannot suppress her desire for a papoose whose "eyes are so black" (308). The eye, the cir-cle of the soul, reflects the spaces both within and without the human being. We call the poet or the visionary a seer because we see the eye as the vehicle of the imagination. This eye Laura looks into, further-more, is black, the presence of all colors, emblematic for the white child of the mysterious "other."[4] Dreaming about the papoose, savoring the word, and eventually looking deeply into the black eyes of a real papoose, Laura in this novel moves toward replacing her father as the seer and storyteller[5] of the *Little House* books, storing images of solitude, space, wilderness, mystery, and freedom as they surround a little house.

TENSION IN STYLE AND STRUCTURE

As I point out in Chapter 3, places, animals, people, things, and actions in *Little House on the Prairie* exist on a continuum from wild to civilized, becoming demonic or chaotic at either extreme. The primary tension in this novel is between the little house and the immense prairie, but the continuum extends in one direction to town (overwhelming civilization) and in the other direction to the creek suddenly full of floodwaters or to a prairie fire raging out of control (overwhelming wilderness). As in all the *Little House* books, Wilder plays with oppositions that humans, especially westerners, perceive as sources of conflict: in this case between nature and human, wilderness and civilization, Native Americans and white settlers, male and female, child and adult, individual and community, younger and older siblings, domesticated and wild animals, construction tools and a fiddle, a bake-oven and a china figurine, a campfire meal and a Christmas dinner, music and stillness, journeying and being at home, building a home and seeing a home threatened. The little house is sometimes not safe, the prairie does sometimes overwhelm, and chaos does sometimes replace the circle; but a balance—tension—is maintained between opposites. This is true even in the title of the book, a balance between "little house" and "prairie."

BALANCING POLARITIES BY STRUCTURE

This balance is perhaps most readily apparent in the structure of the novel. It begins with a departure from the little house in the big woods and ends with a departure from the little house on the prairie. The first word of the title of both the first and the last chapters is "going": "Going West" and "Going Out." In the early drafts of the manuscript, these two titles were "Going In" and "Going Out." The story is about a journey to and then away from a place, but without any clear destination in either case.

As a journey in time, the story is also circular. It covers one cycle of the seasons, beginning and ending in spring, which occupies seven of the twenty-six chapters. As *Little House in the Big Woods* is a winter's tale, this novel is a summer story, dedicating fourteen of its chapters to summer and only two and a half each to fall and winter. In the first novel, winter kept Laura indoors and the warmth, intimacy, and security of the little house were celebrated; summer frees Laura in this novel to play on the prairie and experience its warmth, intimacy, and immensity.

It is true that fall and winter also keep Laura indoors in this novel. But because of the fire in the chimney, Pa's four-day trip to Independence, and the intrusion of several Native Americans, this little house is not the snug, cozy one Laura had in the big woods. When spring returns, the prairie becomes more dangerous than it was in summer, when the house was being built. The Native Americans meet night after night, expressing their rage in loud cries, and a prairie fire sweeps down on the little house. There is by far less security in *Little House on the Prairie* than in *Little House in the Big Woods*.

All this is simply a lack of security. Nothing tragic happens. No one is seriously hurt. No one dies. The only animals that die are killed to be eaten. The little house is still standing on the prairie when the Ingallses depart. Still, the possibility of tragedy is raised. There are threats to the health, safety, and lives of the Ingalls family. Most of these occur in the second half of the novel.

The first half—Chapters 1 through 13—is about building a home. From the raising of the walls to the acquisition of a cow, the house increasingly becomes a home. In eight of these thirteen chapters, there is no danger. And at first, when danger does occur, it occurs outside the house: in crossing the creek, when they are nearly swept away; in raising the walls of the house, when a log falls on Ma and injures her foot; and in digging the well, both when Pa must rescue Mr. Scott (who goes down without first sending a lighted candle to see if the air is good) and when water suddenly floods the well while Pa is at the bottom. But discomfort is experienced and danger is feared when the two Native Americans in skunk skins enter the house to have Ma cook them some food. This is the first time in the *Little House* books that potential danger actually enters a little house. Later in Chapter 13, "Indian Camp," although there is no danger, Laura is taken out onto the prairie on foot and experiences its immensity and her own smallness more intensely than before. Even though the camp is empty and the day is a wonderful outing for the girls, this chapter also serves to remind us of the major threat of the novel—the Native American presence, hidden in the hollows of the prairie.

The second half of the novel, Chapters 14 to 26, is about the testing or threatening of the little house. In "Fever 'n' Ague," all of the family contract malaria, alternating between fevers and chills, hurting, feeling dizzy and weak, and requiring nursing by Mrs. Scott and Dr. Tan. In the next chapter, a high wind causes the stick-and-daub chimney to catch on fire: Ma has to knock it down, and Laura has to pull Mary and Carrie away from the burning sticks that fall out onto the floor under the rocking chair where they are sitting. Then "Pa Goes to Town" and is gone four days, leaving the family to worry that he will get hurt, that he will not be able to return, and that they will have to carry on without him; at the same time, the Native Americans return and begin to make strange noises in the night. In the next chapter, Native Americans are constantly appearing; Soldat du Chêne eats and smokes with Pa, but bad Native Americans steal food, tobacco, and very nearly take Pa's furs from trapping and hunting, which he intends to sell for a plow.

Chapter 19 starts tensely, with the girls' fear that Santa will not find them, though it becomes a chapter reminiscent of the big woods—describing the warmth, fullness, and wonder of Christmas with a loving family and sufficient means. The four chapters that follow this brief respite intensify the danger experienced in Chapters 15 through 18. Rather than a fire in the chimney, here the Ingallses confront a prairie fire. Rather than Native Americans in and around the house, some good and some thieves, now there are large numbers of Native Americans—perhaps Cheyenne, Sioux, and Arapaho as well as Osage—gathering, arguing about the settlers, and (in Chapter 23) making horrifying war cries. But in the last three chapters, danger disappears. Soldat du Chêne wins the day, the Native Americans ride away, and just as suddenly—Pa having heard that soldiers are coming to take the settlers out of Indian Territory—the Ingallses themselves ride away. There has been no danger, then, in five of the thirteen chapters in the second half of the novel.

In other words, the two halves are like mirror images of each other. Eight of the first thirteen chapters are about the little house; eight of the last thirteen are about the prairie. The ratio of danger to safety is five to eight in the first half; eight to five in the last half. The second half balances four chapters of danger against four later chapters of more intense danger. What was originally only two Native Americans in the house steadily becomes a larger and larger threat until the possibility of war emerges in Chapter 23, "Indian War-Cry." In the first half, Pa builds a home; in the second half, illness, fire, a panther, and Native Americans threaten it. Although not completely idyllic, the first half woos us with the safety of the house and the beauty of the prairie. The last half clearly descends into a demonic world, as the Ingallses spend night after night terrified by the yelling Native Americans, to be released finally by the heroic "tall Indian."

In all this, "romance" structure is obvious. For one thing, adults seen from a young child's viewpoint are larger than life, either heroes or villains. But more important, Wilder clearly designs the plot to create a circular journey from an idyllic world with problems into a demonic world and then back to the idyllic world, now transformed.

ANTITHESIS AND BALANCE IN STYLE

Contrasting parallels achieve not only structural balance but also stylistic balance. Words, phrases, clauses, and sentences often have the same form but contrasting meanings. The title *Little House in the Big Woods* is an obvious example, "little" contrasting with "big," "house" with "woods," but the form is the same for both—adjective followed by a noun. In parallelism, similarity in form links two words or groups of words and invites us to look at them together. Doing so, we can see and stress differences while holding both sides together as a whole. *Little House on the Prairie* is obviously parallel to *Little House in the Big Woods*, although to say "big prairie" here would be redundant. The titles of the series as a whole rely on contrasting parallelism or antithesis. *On the Banks of Plum Creek* is parallel to *By the Shores of Silver Lake; Farmer Boy* is parallel to *The Long Winter;* and *Little Town on the Prairie* is parallel to *Little House on the Prairie. These Happy Golden Years* breaks the parallelism in titles (if not in structure) and ends the series.

Some of the chapter titles of *Little House on the Prairie* also are parallel but contrasting. I have already noted "Going West" and "Going Out." In addition, there are "Camp on the High Prairie" and "The House on the Prairie"; "The House on the Prairie" and "Indians in the House"; "A Fire on the Hearth" and "Fire in the Chimney"; "Indian Jamboree" and "Indian War-Cry." Here, too, the differences expressed in parallel forms draw our attention to what is different and let us hold contrasting images together as part of a whole.

In "The Symbolic Center," I pointed out Wilder's preference for "and" rather than "but," and for prepositions such as "in" and "on." She uses these words to unite rather than oppose very different things. This preference is evident in *Little House on the Prairie.* So is her tendency to use both mythic and realistic conventions of storytelling. This novel opens:

> A long time ago, when all the grandfathers and grandmothers of today were little boys and little girls or very small babies, or perhaps not even born, Pa and Ma and Mary and Laura and Baby Carrie left their little house in the Big Woods of Wisconsin. They drove away and left it lonely and empty in the clearing among the big trees, and they never saw that little house again.
>
> They were going to the Indian country.
>
> Pa said there were too many people in the Big Woods now. Quite often Laura heard the ringing thud of an ax which was not Pa's ax, or the echo of a shot that did not come from his gun. The

path that went by the little house had become a road. Almost every day Laura and Mary stopped their playing and stared in surprise at a wagon slowly creaking by on that road.

Wild animals would not stay in a country where there were so many people. Pa did not like to stay, either. He liked a country where the wild animals lived without being afraid. He liked to see the little fawns and their mothers looking at him from the shadowy woods, and the fat, lazy bears in the wild-berry patches.

In the long winter evenings he talked to Ma about the Western country. In the West the land was level, and there were no trees. The grass grew thick and high. There the wild animals wandered and fed as though they were in a pasture that stretched much farther than a man could see, and there were no settlers. Only Indians lived there. (1–2)

In these five brief paragraphs, "and" is used fifteen times—nine times in the first paragraph alone. One effect of "and" is to give each item equal weight and attention, to focus on each item and on connections between items; in other words, to be mindful. Another effect is to achieve balance—to hold these things in tension. Often items are similar and yet opposite, for example, "grandfathers and grandmothers," "little boys and little girls," "Pa and Ma," "Mary and Laura."

"A long time ago" is a typical fairy tale opening. A contrasting, realistic (that is, historical) explanation of "a long time ago" follows immediately—"when all the grandfathers and grandmothers of today were little." The first opening uses general language that appeals to an audience of all ages; the second serves to clarify the first for an audience of children. It explains "a long time ago" in terms that children can understand and might even use themselves. The second sentence merely repeats in parallel form the last half of the first sentence, substituting "they" for the Ingallses' names, because they have already been specified, and focusing on the little house, giving us a specific picture of it as "lonely and empty" and abandoned.

The next paragraph is only one general sentence about their goal. It contrasts sharply with the first and third paragraphs in topic (they are about the settled big woods) and in length. Its brevity makes it stand out despite its generality. Indeed, we must pause in the midst of sentences that rush on to ponder what "Indian country" is like. We must also notice the opposition between "they" (the Ingalls family, already carefully identified in the first sentence of the book) and "Indian."

Then the third paragraph returns to the little house to explain why they left. Again the pattern is a generalization, "Pa said there were too many people in the Big Woods now," followed by specifics that children will understand, largely because they are from Laura's point of view and experience—the sounds of axes or guns and the sight of wagons passing. Here, too, there is contrast in specifics: between the sound of Pa's ax and gun and the sounds of other people's, between the path and the road, between Laura's and Mary's playing and "a wagon slowly creaking by on the road." The image of the wagon going by the Ingalls house also refers us back to the first paragraph, where we are told that the Ingalls drove away, presumably in "a wagon slowly creaking by" other little houses on this road.

The fourth paragraph provides a transition from images of the big woods to images of the prairie, introducing wild animals in opposition to people. The problem with the big woods is that "wild animals would not stay in a country where there were so many people." The next sentence, nearly parallel in form, contrasts Pa with "so many people" and implicitly identifies him with the wild animals: "Pa did not like to stay, either." The next two sentences, parallel in form ("He liked . . . He liked") follow the pattern of moving from the general to the specific, that is, from unafraid wild animals to "fawns and their mothers looking at him" and "fat, lazy bears in wild-berry patches."

Finally, in the fifth paragraph, we catch a glimpse of "Indian country." It seems only a vision because it is largely defined by absence—of hills, trees, people—and as endless pasture. Although less concrete than the images of deer and bear in the preceding sentences, the image of thick, high grass where wild animals wander and feed reminds me of Emily Dickinson's poem:

> To make a prairie it takes a clover and one bee,
> One clover, and one bee,
> And revery.

> The revery alone will do,
> If bees are few.

Pa's prairie is a dream image—a creation of revery. This image is exploded again by a short, general statement: "Only Indians lived there." Given Pa's dislike of there being many people, we must wonder here why Native Americans are not a problem for him. They must not frighten away the wild animals as do the settlers. By implication, like Pa, they must be like the wild animals and unlike settlers or, as the fourth paragraph suggests, unlike people.

REPETITION

Often, repetition with variation serves the same function as contrasts in parallel form. Repetition with variation is found, for example, in the titles of the first and last chapters: "Going West," "Going Out." It also appears in sentences: "Wild animals did not like to stay in a country where there were so many people" and "Pa did not like to stay either"; "He liked a country" and "He liked to see." In the opening paragraphs of the book, the first, third and fourth paragraphs are about the big woods: one focuses on leaving the woods, one on why the Ingallses are going, and one on how the big woods used to be. Also, the second and fifth paragraphs are both about "Indian country": the second paragraph is merely one very general sentence, but the fifth is longer and more specific, though still leaving room for the imagination.

The structure itself also shows repetition with variation. I have pointed out how many chapters are about danger, but this danger can come from something outside the house (wolves, fire, Native Americans) or from something inside (illness, fire, and Native Americans). Several chapters deal with the same subject but in different forms: water in different forms, fire in different forms, poor health as injury or illness, wild animals as wolves or panther, and Native Americans in many different scenes.

Repetition with variation, then, also functions to balance contrasting images.

SYMBOLISM

The key to the style and structure of *Little House on the Prairie* is antithesis, or contrast and balance—in diction, images, sentences, chapters, and larger parts of the novel. Antithesis may be achieved through contrasting but parallel words, characters, settings, or events, or through repetition with variation. Wilder's attention to detail encourages us to stay in the moment and experience fully whatever is happening; and her careful stylistic and structural patterning encourages us to evaluate everything in relation to one or more other things. The effect is to create powerful symbols, vivid images radiating with meaning that resonate long after the reader finishes the book. The little house and the prairie, the settler and the Native American, people and wild animals, Ma and Pa, Mary and Laura, baby Carrie and Laura, building a house and threats to a house—all these are symbols, along with many others.

POINTS, CIRCLES, AND CHAOS

The overall structure of the novel comprises contrasting worlds, creating what Northrop Frye identifies as the structure of romance.[6] This is a circular journey from the big woods to the prairie, to a little house on a prairie, to a little house beset by danger, to a little house freed of danger, to a journey on the prairie. As I have emphasized, a magic circle controls the structure of this novel and keeps the Ingallses safe.

According to Ralph Abraham in *Chaos—Gaia—Eros: A Chaos Pioneer Uncovers the Three Great Streams of History,* the circle is an old symbol. It began to dominate human society around 3500 B.C.—when the wheel was invented—humanity having by then come to understand "periodic processes, such as the cycle of the seasons, the menstrual cycle, the phases of the moon, and the daily solar cycle."[7] Abraham identifies the first epoch of history as the "static" age, beginning about 9000 B.C., when the development of agriculture "defeated the chaos of nature by stabilizing the wanderers in homeostasis, a static state" (62). The second epoch is the "periodic" age associated with the wheel and representing a system in oscillation. The third is the "chaotic" age, begun in A.D. 1961 and associated with "fractal (infinitely folded) sets of states, over which the model system moves, occupying different states in a sequence called a *trajectory* . . . [which,] while appearing irregular or random, actually progresses in a deterministic manner" (60). These ages, based on mathematical models, are determined by different "attractors"—"special forms of dynamical behaviors . . . [of] three types . . . static, periodic, and chaotic" (60). Static attractors are also known as "point" attractors and represent a system at rest; periodic attractors "consist of a cycle of states, repeated again and again, always in the same period of time" (60). Chaotic attractors display features of order and disorder, representing "systems in states of agitation, as in the case of turbulence" (60).

I find Abraham's analysis helpful for understanding the structure of the *Little House* books. In *Little House in the Big Woods,* the little house is a static attractor, and thus we have a system at rest—a little house in winter. In *Little House on the Prairie,* the prairie is a periodic attractor, so that we have a cycle of states: the presence and absence of Pa and of the Native Americans, and the beginnings of the journeys to and from the prairie, all associated with daily and seasonal cycles. In *On the Banks of Plum Creek,* the creek, the dugout, the plague of grasshoppers covering prairie and house, and Laura's temper are chaotic attractors, and we have turbulence that seems like complete disorder.

Despite the dominance of one kind of attractor, however, each of these books offers examples of all three. In the first *Little House* book, for example, there is the cycle of the seasons—a periodic attractor which gives the novel some movement and some assurance of predictability. Laura's temper is also a chaotic attractor, as in the episode when the shopkeeper admires Mary's blond curls but not Laura's brown ones. In *Little House on the Prairie,* not surprisingly, the little house also serves as a static attractor, though it is not entirely successful; and there is a long list of chaotic attractors, including the wild water in the creek and the well, the fire in the chimney and on the prairie, the wolves and the panther, the prairie in stormy weather or without Pa, the Native Americans crying for war, and the blackness of the papoose's eyes.

Static and periodic attractors are comfortable for us because they offer security. Either they assure us of "a symbolic center" or a sacred wellspring of life, as in the first of Wilder's books, or they assure us of repetition and thereby of some control over our lives. The circle—the wheel—is safe movement. It is for this reason that "in the mythology and religious images [of western civilization] . . . we've seen it as a primary sacred symbol. To Plato the circle represented divine perfection. . . . The medicine wheel and other circular metaphors abound in sacred literature" (Abraham, 166–67). The circle, the cycle, makes possible what Mircea Eliade calls the "eternal return."[8] An ordered universe, a cosmos, guarantees that there is no end because every apparent end begins another cycle. In light of myths of an eternal cosmos and eternal return, linear history and death are, therefore, not real.

THE LINE

This brings us to the line as a pattern of organization. In *Little House on the Prairie,* the Ingallses go west in accordance with the myth of "manifest destiny": as the frontier moved west, so did American pioneers, settling the land and building the country. The Ingallses follow a road—a line—until they come to the high prairie. Then "no road, not even the faintest trace of wheels or of a rider's passing, could be seen anywhere. That prairie looked as if no human eye had ever seen it before. Only the tall grass covered the endless empty land and a great empty sky arched over it" (26). Laura sees the wagon as the moving center of a circle, and this may work against our perception of the line, but the line is there—as it was in American history. The line was often claimed to be a line of progress, conquering the wilderness and coming to an end only when there was no longer a frontier. By 1930, the United States was a settled country stretching from the Atlantic to the Pacific ocean.

One problem with the line as a symbol is that it implies a clear beginning and ending. The little house is made of lines, mostly horizontal, defining it as the opposite of the circular prairie and sky. The

Native American trail Laura discovers hidden in the tall grasses seems endless, but will prove finite later in the novel, when the "Indians Ride Away." Lines define what humans build; nature is rounded. Especially important, the lines emphasized in this novel go from east to west, from where the sun rises to where it sets, from symbolic birth and beginning to symbolic death and ending. The frontier, of course, disappeared. When the Native Americans are pushed west one more time, their line of departure speaks volumes about their loss of space and their movement toward death—not only personal death but the end of their way of life. Thus, although a line remains more predictable than chaos, its association with progress is undercut when its direction is from east to west, and because it always implies an ending.

DISORDER AND CHAOS

We feel threatened by loss of order and loss of control. When nature becomes unpredictable, we know we may be in danger. Swollen creeks, prairie fires, storms, marauding panthers—all these are dangerous, and they are even more dangerous for inexperienced pioneers. Disorder also threatens when humans don't behave according to the rules of civility. Horse thieves, for example, leave a couple stranded on the prairie with the wagon holding all their worldly possessions: they are unwilling to leave it and go to Independence with the Ingallses; they didn't have a dog to warn them of thieves or a chain to secure their horses (328–30). Rage also produces disorder or chaos, as when the Native Americans cry for war.

We are frightened by disorder—by chaos—and we think of it as bad or evil. That is one implication of this novel, though the novel implies primarily that chaos is dangerous. On the other hand, Abraham tells us that "in Hesiod, chaos is the gap between heaven and earth; one of the fundamental forces . . . , a state of disorder, [or] in chaos theory, a dynamical system that is neither static nor periodic" (235).

Abraham explores the "periodic" age, the metaphor of the cycle, and the "dominator paradigm" upheld in western civilization by religion and science. In the "dominator paradigm," everything has its place in the order of things—a hierarchy with God at the top and Satan at the bottom. Below God come the angels; then rich white men; then their white wives; then their children; then rich men of color and their wives and children; then middle-class white men; and so on, down to the vegetables and minerals. Age, disability, sexual orientation, and other bases for discrimination also affect the order. The point is that those at the top have power over the system and dominate it. In every situation, someone takes charge of the "other."

This system—characterized by sexism, racism, classism, ageism, ableism, heterosexism, and the destruction of nature—is under attack these days. Many people, like Abraham, believe that grasping for order and control is inherently damaging to the "other" and ultimately to the self.[9] They see the opposition of chaos against order, nature against humans, women against men, and children against adults as false dichotomies and envision a "chaos revolution" that will replace patriarchy with partnership: "a renewal of creativity in the arts, a striving for the rights of women and of animals, for the preservation of the environment, and for peace between nations and people" (Abraham, 73; see also 150 and 220). When we define "reality" in terms of chaos attractors, we see a huge interdependent system in which change in any part will affect the whole.

Abraham ends his book with a warning that "conservative forces [are] at work to protect the dominator paradigm" (220). He believes that if these forces succeed, it will be the "end of history for the human race." He argues for Paul Tillich's view of "two human tendencies—the anxious, conservative attraction to the past and the courageous, revolutionary attraction to the future—as the fundamental dynamic of history, and the realization of the divine. *The creativity of chaos stands between these forces, of the past and of the future.*"[10]

In *Little House on the Prairie*, Ma represents "the anxious, conservative attraction to the past"; Pa, "the courageous, revolutionary attraction to the future"; and Laura, "the creativity of chaos [that] stands between." Circles of varying size keep Laura safe here, but the prairie, wild water and fire, the wolves and the panther, the Native Americans, and the blackness of the papoose's eyes confront Laura with chaos and nourish her imagination. In *Little House in the Big Woods,* we see how her mindfulness can expand the little house. In *Little House on the Prairie,* we see how it can make the endless prairie a home. Here she learns for herself what Pa's stories all suggest: Adventure is worth the fear and the risk. In *On the Banks of Plum Creek* and in the later books, especially *The Long Winter,* she will find that chaos can defeat and destroy but that it always teaches her something about herself that allows her to survive and grow. Here, she has learned the importance of freedom and openness to change. The endless prairie bores Laura when she first views it from the covered wagon, but when they leave the little house on the prairie, she is "all excited inside [because] you never know what will happen next, nor where you'll be tomorrow, when you are traveling in a covered wagon" (327).

5

The Mythic Journey: How to Live

FUNCTIONS OF MYTH

If the structure of *Little House on the Prairie* is mythic, what are its larger meanings? What are the implications of its symbolic images and patterns? Joseph Campbell identifies four functions of myth: (1) mystical, or experiencing awe before the mystery and wonder of the universe; (2) cosmological, or explaining the shape and origin of creation; (3) sociological, or "supporting and validating a certain social order"; and (4) pedagogical, or explaining "how to live life under any circumstances."[1]

In this chapter, I explore some of the novel's religious implications, in the context of the whole series.[2] In Campbell's terms, I examine its cosmological, mystical, and pedagogical functions as myth. In Chapter 6, I examine its personal or psychological implications for understanding Laura as the character who grows up in the *Little House* books; these too are mythic and serve what Campbell identifies as the pedagogical function, especially as he analyzes it in *The Hero with a Thousand Faces.*[3] In Chapter 7, I analyze this novel and the series in terms of their sociological function as American myth.

Cosmological Function

It would seem logical to examine *Little House on the Prairie* in terms of its author's Christianity. Certainly, Northrop Frye's understanding of literature as centered in myth, displacing its mythic structure as it ranges from romance to realistic fiction, rests largely on his knowledge of the Bible and Christianity.[4] His pattern for the demonic world is clearly hell; his pattern for the idyllic world is heaven. Christ is the hero (God) who goes into the wilderness (the demonic world, life, death, hell); defeats Satan (the monster); harrows (vivifies, transforms) hell; and rises to the idyllic world (heaven). Knowing that the Ingallses were Christian, western readers might see Pa or Laura or the white settlers as heroes (Jesus figures) going into a world of wild spaces, animals, and people (hell), defeating bad or monstrous people (Satan), and harrowing (cleansing, planting) this wilderness, transforming it into civilization (heaven).

The novel does evolve out of the stark oppositions characteristic of Christianity, western culture, and patriarchy. But rather than elevate one side over the other, Wilder balances opposites, emphasizing the worth of each. In other words, there is no sharp contrast between good and evil. Christianity is alluded to only once, when Laura asks if Jack, who seems to have been killed when they crossed the creek, "can't go to heaven" (27) and Pa responds, "God that doesn't forget the sparrows won't leave a good dog like Jack out in the cold" (27). In the later books, it becomes apparent that the Ingallses are Congregationalists of the more liberal kind (like the Reverend Mr. Alden), rather than the evangelical kind (like the Reverend Mr. Brown). However, the respect and love for animals indicated by this conversation about Jack—along with other images—suggest a different cosmology. In this regard, then, Campbell's approach seems more useful than Frye's.

Campbell ranges freely over the myths and scriptures of the world, using eastern religions and Native American spirituality to correct what he sees as faults of Christianity.[5] He holds that the creation story told in Genesis 2—the story of Adam and Eve's fall and their loss of the Garden of Eden—divides nature and life from God and paradise, thereby condemning nature and life as imperfect, defiled, transitory, and sinful (*Power,* 47–49). Alan Watts (in *The Wisdom of Insecurity*) explains at some length that this division provided an impetus for the enlightenment and the development of science, which in turn further divided God from humanity and humanity from nature. Descartes' *cognito ergo sum* ("I think; therefore, I am") separated "I" (subject) from everything else (object)—for example, from his own body, nature, a female, a person of color, a person with a disability, a younger or an older person, or anyone with any other difference. In effect, Watts says, "It's as if we were divided into two parts . . . , the conscious 'I,' at once intrigued and baffled, the creature who is caught in a trap . . . , [and] me, . . . a part of nature—the wayward flesh with all its concurrently beautiful and frustrating limitations" (39).

Watts argues that such a division ensures perpetual conflict, violence, and war between "I" and "me" (115). Campbell identifies this struggle with the "imperialistic thrust" of Judaism, Christianity, and Islam (21). Division separates us, isolates us, and engenders fear. It invites comparison, evaluation, and struggles for power as a means of feeling secure. It results in an "in-group" opposed to all those who are "out," that is, those who do not believe in or are more distant than "I" from the "one, true God." It has resulted in patriarchy, in technology (the wheel), and in increasingly destructive wars for the purpose of converting and colonizing the infidel.[6]

Wilder's strategy, however, is to connect opposites, not divide them. It is Mary *and* Laura, Ma *and* Pa, white settler *and* Native American, little house *and* prairie. Laura has her preferences—for Pa, for being outdoors on the prairie, for the papoose, for living like an "Indian girl"—but the reader, through Laura, sees that there is good in Mary, Ma, white settlers, and little house. (This is also, and especially, true in the later books.) *Little House on the Prairie* assumes that cooperation will occur because everyone and everything—particularly nature—has value and deserves respect. The novel's cosmology seems closer to eastern or Native American religions than to traditional Christianity.

I take seriously Campbell's claim that we need a "mythology of the planet—and we don't have such a mythology. The closest thing I know to a planetary mythology is Buddhism, which sees all beings as Buddha beings. The only problem is to come to a recognition of that. There is nothing to do. The task is only to know what is, and then to act in relation to the brotherhood of all of these beings" (*Power,* 22). I make no claim that this novel embodies *the* mythology of the planet. I do claim, however, it offers *a* mythology for the planet.

I introduce one version of this mythology in Chapter 1, in the discussion of wilderness. Another version appears in Chapter 4, in my discussion of Ralph Abraham and others who see the universe (usually focusing on the Earth) as an interdependent system in process, with some parts at rest and some in periodic motion—seemingly chaotic and definitely imperfect but abundantly creative and, it is to be hoped, headed toward a peace best characterized as partnership between its parts. These parts can be broadly seen as the environment, people, and nations, and narrowly as all the dualities characteristic of western thought. The goal is the reunion of the parts into a whole, each aware of and respectful of every other.

Interestingly, Native American spirituality, eastern religions, and liberal Christian theology, especially process theology, provide other versions of this mythology. Campbell addresses the first two. Watts expands on Campbell's discussion of eastern religions as a source of mythology for the west. There are many writers who examine Native American mythologies as a remedy for our times, especially for the ecological crisis.[7] In addition, liberal Christianity reimagines the story of Jesus, and process theology reimagines the nature of God; thus in varying degrees, depending on the theologian, we get another version of this mythology of the planet.[8] The call for partnership is, of course, the main theme of feminist theologians, partnership with the earth, of ecofeminists.[9]

The Mystical Function

In all religions, there are mystics, people who see or experience everything as oneness—Hindu yogis, Tantric and Zen Buddhists, Taoists, cabalistic Jews, Sufi Muslims, many Roman Catholic saints, and shamans of the primal religions of southeast Asia, Siberia, the Americas, the Pacific Islands, Australia, and Africa.[10] Chapter 42 of the *Tao Te Ching* provides an eastern mystic's paradoxical cosmology:

> Tao gives birth to the One.
> The One gives birth to Two.
> Two gives birth to Three.
> Three gives birth to all things.

> All things have their back to the female
> and stand facing the male.
> When male and female combine,
> all things achieve harmony.

> Ordinary men hate solitude.
> But the Master makes use of it,
> embracing his aloneness, realizing
> he is one with the whole universe.[11]

Similarly, in primal religions everything is sacred and one. In *Sacred Earth,* Versluis identifies the Native American experience of nature as theophany or divine revelation.[12] In Versluis's words, "For indigenous peoples in particular . . . virgin nature is sacred. Everything in the natural world embodies spiritual truth" (12). Open to this truth, immersed in a place, free of any sense of self, caught up in the great mystery or in the flow of reality, the mystic experiences the one as the many, the many as the one, and the present moment as eternal.

Watts asks us to think about our own experience when we are fully involved in some activity. He points out that our experience of reality is oneness. There are no separate "experiencers" and no separate experiences we can stand outside of. As soon as we start to think about experiencing reality, we are no longer experiencing; instead, we are resisting the experience by thinking about it. Still, we are then at one with the thinking. We are not separate from the thinking; there is no thought we can stand outside of. Hard as we might try, we cannot step outside; and as long as we keep trying, we are caught in a vicious circle. Watts confirms the mystic's experience. We are not separate.

Reality is one. The notion of two or three or many is a convention of language, thought, and memory. Furthermore, reality is always unknown, always changing, always dying and being born each moment, and always all that there is—that is, eternal. Whatever we call our experience—God, the sacred, the divine, ultimate reality, the ground of being—it is one and beyond words, thoughts, or memories. It is always the present, eternal moment.

The Pedagogical Function

One of Watts's themes in *The Wisdom of Insecurity* is that we have forgotten that language, thoughts, beliefs, science, and memories are only metaphors or symbols for reality. This is also one of Campbell's themes, although I think he never explains it as clearly as Watts. Asked by Bill Moyers why we think in terms of opposites, Campbell responds, "Because we can't think otherwise" (*Power*, 49), and later adds that "the ultimate mystery of being is beyond all categories of thought" (49).

Watts supplies the explanation when he describes all thought and language as relative, that is, based on comparison with something else. We can't talk about the one, eternal reality. We can talk of anything only in terms of something else. For example, we explain good in terms of evil, man in terms of woman, God in terms of human beings, the supernatural in terms of the natural. Watts reminds us that language and thought are not reality, but only representations of reality—metaphors or symbols. Like Campbell and many contemporary Christian theologians, Watts holds that all theology is metaphorical and warns against mistaking it for reality.[13] In Campbell's words, when people are "stuck with their metaphor and don't realize its reference[,] . . . [t]hey haven't allowed the circle that surrounds them to open. It is a closed circle" (*Power*, 21), what Watts calls a "vicious circle."

Fear, suffering, and denial result from living in our heads and mistaking our thoughts and memories for reality. Viewed dualistically, life is frightfully insecure. We have no control over the future, no assurance that even the next moment will turn out as we planned (Fleck, 146). We experience reality as flux and chaos, bringing loss, sorrow, and death. No matter how hard we try, we cannot predict its pattern, and we cannot fix it in place. The lesson, clearly, is to quit trying. Fleck calls for letting go and acceptance; Watts and the eastern mystics call for "being completely sensitive to each moment," that is, mindful (95). Native American mythology calls for being open to nature as an expression of the divine. All point out that loveliness, joy, liveliness, love, creativity, challenges, and the blessings of life exist precisely because life is insecure, imperfect, and impermanent. Paradoxically, it is when we let go and are mindful of the moment that we become complete and secure. We experience the wisdom of insecurity and the blessings of imperfection—what the Buddhists call "enlightenment."

A MYTHIC JOURNEY

"As a Little Child"

Campbell identifies the two principal mythic images as "the simple, innocent, childlike one, and the terrific threat" (*Power*, 17). He says that everyone learns religious and mythic ideas "as a child on one level," but then, as we mature, "many different levels are revealed. Myths are infinite in their revelations" (*Power*, 148). In *Little House on the Prairie*, Laura Ingalls Wilder tells of her experience as a little girl. We enter the experience from her viewpoint, that of a small child who does not see herself as separate from her family or from the world. The result is that we experience, as she does, the oneness of reality—a version of paradise, heaven, eternity, or the ground of being.

As I imply in Chapter 4, Laura's view of the prairie tells us as much about her as it does about the prairie. When she is afraid because Pa is gone or the Native Americans are crying out, she experiences the prairie as threatening, and she stays in the house. She separates herself from the prairie, projecting her fearfulness onto it. In Watts's terms, she divides reality in an attempt to feel secure. At the beginning of the novel, she does the same thing when she is bored by the prairie—she projects her boredom onto it and separates herself from it, complaining and asking her parents to stop. She experiences herself and the covered wagon as trapped at the center of a circle of prairie that never changes (*LHP,* 13). Clearly, this is what Campbell would call a closed circle and Watts would call a vicious circle.

Still, our primary experience in the novel is of mindfulness, as explained in Chapter 3. Laura and the reader are completely immersed in the people, places, things, and events of the novel. We are at one, as we are in *Little House in the Big Woods.* Both novels make me think of Jesus's words: "Whoever does not receive the kingdom of God as a little child will never enter it" (Mark 10:15).

Of course, these two novels do differ in their focus. The first identifies Laura with the little house; the second identifies her with the prairie. *Little House in the Big Woods* is static. It is about the symbolic center, the source of life, power, and illumination. It is about Laura's basic trust in life as she experiences it in the little house with her family—especially Pa and Jack, who keep her safe from the big woods; but also Ma, who makes the house a home. As a storyteller and fiddler, Pa also makes the house a window on the world, nourishing his daughters'—especially Laura's—imagination. *Little House on the Prairie* is about the journey to and from Kansas: that is, about a circular movement. It is about safe, predictable, periodic motion that is sometimes a trap, frequently threatens to break up into chaos, but also releases Laura and the reader from the circle to moments of transcendence.

Leaving the First Little House

The novel begins with one little house left "lonely and empty in the clearing among the big trees" (*LHP,* 1). This little house, which was the central image of *Little House in the Big Woods,* vividly symbolizes Laura's security—here expressed as a place filled with all the people and things she needs to be safe and happy. In the opening pages, we hear in detail about what happens to this little house: the cow and calf are sold; the girls are dressed in several layers of wool and coats, hoods, and mittens; the house is emptied and the wagon is loaded; good-byes are said; the Ingallses get into the wagon; and "they all went away from the little log house. The shutters were over the windows, so the little house could not see them go. It stayed there inside the log fence, behind the two big oak trees that in summertime had made green roofs for Mary and Laura to play under. And that was the last of the little house" (6).

Pa directs Laura's attention toward the future with the promise that she will see a papoose. Still, she doesn't like crossing Lake Pepin, and she expresses relief when there are again trees and earth. She feels better, we are told, because "there was a little log house, too, among the trees" (7). Obviously, leaving the little house in the big woods is unsettling, even frightening.

The Journey to the Prairie

Laura is frightened by Pa's talk about the ice breaking the day after they have crossed it, and then we find that the journey requires many crossings of water and also getting wet in the rain—water serving here (as it does in many religious rituals) to initiate Laura into a new life.

Laura's boredom with endless Kansas follows. Next, they are at great risk as they cross the flooded creek, and they lose Jack. Mary obediently lies still as they cross, but Laura sits up and looks. She sees Pa in the water with the horses and sees that Ma's face is "white and scared" (23). She lies down when Ma orders her to do so and experiences her first real fear for her life as a cold sickness. When the wagon is on the ground again, Laura is once again up, looking. She realizes that if any of the family had behaved differently, they would have been drowned (24). Then she discovers that they have lost Jack.

The camp on the high prairie in Chapter 3 restores some sense of home, as careful attention is paid to building a fire, preparing a meal, and getting ready for bed. Then Jack returns, and "all's well that ends well," as Pa says repeatedly in this novel. The next chapter—about a day of rest in camp—continues our sense of a journey's end and of settling in. The Ingallses are back in the wagon and on the move again in Chapter 5, but only for a short distance, to the site of the new house on the prairie.

Homemaking

Once again, a little house becomes the focus. But this novel is not about being at home, but rather about building and furnishing a home. Instead of stasis, we experience nearly constant activity. Finding this place has been a result of activity (in Chapters 1 to 6), and Pa now erects the walls of the house and stable, makes strong doors, puts on a roof, lays a floor, digs a well, and procures a cow and calf. Laura watches closely and tells us about the process. This shift away from place and toward action continues.

Pa as Teacher

As in *Little House in the Big Woods,* Pa is Laura's favorite parent, the one she identifies with. As a mythic image, he is her guide (mentor, shaman) on this journey—a journey that in its entirety can be seen as a vision quest (Versluis, 37–41). As I note in Chapter 4, Pa associates himself with wilderness—with the wild animals and the Native Americans. Laura thinks, "Pa knew about wild animals, so he must know about wild men, too. Laura thought he would show her a papoose some day, just as he had shown her fawns, and little bears, and wolves" (56). Remember that Pa actually names the goal of her quest—the papoose. He is thus a great deal more than a competent pioneer providing for his family and teaching his daughters how to be pioneers. Also, especially with his fiddle, he is a magician, able to transform the wilderness and to reveal its secrets. At the very least, Pa shows respect for wilderness, and sometimes we see him in awe of it and at one with it, responding (like the Native Americans) to animals and landscape as sacred.

A Circle of Wolves

The night the wolves surround the house is a good example of Pa's attitude toward nature. He has his gun, but he doesn't shoot any of the wolves. Instead, he admires them through the window and holds Laura up to see. Like Pa, Laura responds with wonder. One of the novel's most haunting images is created in this passage:

> There in the moonlight sat half a circle of wolves. They sat on their haunches and looked at Laura in the window, and she looked at them. She had never seen such big wolves. The biggest one was taller than Laura. He was taller even than Mary. He sat in the middle, exactly opposite Laura. Everything about him was

big—his pointed ears, and his pointed mouth with the tongue hanging out, and his strong shoulders and legs, and his two paws side by side, and his tail curled around the squatting haunch. His coat was shaggy gray and his eyes were glittering green.

Laura clutched her toes into a crack of the wall and she folded her arms on the window slab, and she looked and looked at that wolf. . . .

"He's awful big," Laura whispered.

"Yes, and see how his coat shines," Pa whispered into her hair. The moonlight made little glitters in the edges of the shaggy fur, all around the big wolf. (96–97)

When the gray wolf howls at the moon, "then all around the house the circle of wolves pointed their noses toward the sky and answered him. Their howls shuddered through the house and filled the moonlight and quavered away across the vast silence of the prairie" (98). Here we experience oneness with the wilderness. Laura's response illuminates and transforms the circle of wolves, putting us in touch with mystery.

In the *Little House in the Big Woods,* Pa was a storyteller; but in this novel, as Laura takes over that function, Pa's role changes. He now becomes Laura's guide to being a pioneer. He is a practical person whose skills make life possible in the wilderness, but he is also her initiator into the mystery and sacredness of wilderness. He shows her its wonders, transforming reality—especially when he expresses his yearning imagination by playing his fiddle.

The Prairie

The prairie is the principal source of mystery and wonder in this novel. As we have seen, the narrator—from Laura's point of view—provides passage after passage of lyrical description. We see all the small animals, birds, flowers, grasses—everything that catches Laura's attention. We hear birds, frogs, grasshoppers, and the ever-present wind. We feel the warm breeze and sun and smell the clean freshness of the prairie. Repeatedly, we experience the openness, vastness, emptiness, and silence of the prairie, and its huge sky (26, 40, 48, 50, 53, 54, 55, 174, 178, 208, 211, 214, 294, 295, 311, 325, 328, 332, and 335).

At night, Laura turns from the huge darkness of the prairie to the moonlight or starlight of the sky. Laura's response to Pa's music guides us to see him as a magician, but it is she herself who sees the stars as low enough for him to pluck one (37) and as singing (51) and dancing (66).

Prairie and sky are images of infinity. They invite us to engage in reverie—to ponder the eternal. Their lack of definition, their emptiness and openness and vastness, reminds me of the Buddhist state of nothingness, emptiness, or void necessary to achieve enlightenment. Also, as the wind blows the grasses, the prairie is always in motion; and this suggests another Buddhist concept—that all is flux. Free of the distractions of the material world, a follower of Buddhism, under a master's guidance, no longer clings to illusions of security but becomes open to mystery, the sacred, oneness, God, reality, enlightenment. Similarly, after Laura leaves behind the little house in the big woods, she experiences the insecurity of the little house on the prairie and, under Pa's guidance, becomes open to wilderness. The prairie is the novel's principal image of wilderness, its principal metaphor for that which is beyond all categories of thought. It is the real hero, the main character, of this novel.

Native Americans

The prairie's true inhabitants are Native Americans. The novel certainly does not romanticize them, any more than it romanticizes the prairie. The prairie is at times frighteningly huge, empty, and silent; and Native Americans smell like skunks, steal, and threaten war. But they also are friendly, dignified peacemakers (Soldat du Chêne) and responsible fathers (one has tracked and killed the panther before Pa could). They may wash clothes in the creek, live on dirt floors with the fire in the center of their tents and a hole above to let smoke out, and wear few or no clothes; but they live in harmony with the prairie, building their camps in its hidden protected hollows, erecting little that will permanently alter the landscape, and moving with the seasons and the wild animals.

As a range of Native Americans present themselves to Laura, she is also presented with a range of opinions about them. The Scotts take an extreme view, based on their knowledge of the Minnesota Massacre and their ideas about the doctrine of manifest destiny. Pa is ambivalent. He admires Native Americans, wants to be at peace with them, and knows they have every reason to be angry; still, he expects them to leave the prairie, although their departure saddens him. Pa seems implicitly to see "Indians" as different from the white settlers and akin to wild animals. But to some extent he identifies with wild animals, and so does Laura. Although Laura is fascinated by the Native Americans, as by the wolves, she is also afraid when two Native American men enter the house near the end of the first half of the novel. Near the end of the second half of the novel, she is terrified during the nights of their preparation for war. She listens to what the adults say and asks questions until the contradictions (including Pa's) become clear. When the Native Americans ride away, besides wishing to be one of them, she expresses the grief that Pa, Ma, and Mary also clearly feel.

This is not meant to defend Wilder against charges of racism. She does not provide us with an inside view, or even a comprehensive outside view, of Native Americans. We know no more than little Laura sees and hears. Native Americans here function merely as symbols, not as fully developed human beings. Akin to wild animals, they are in Laura's eyes wild people (56). As such, like the circle of wolves and the prairie, they represent considerable magic for her. They are another image of mystery and of freedom from civilization's restraints—clothes, tame horses, and stationary homes.

The Papoose's Black Eyes

When Laura locks eyes with the papoose, we arrive at the end of her quest. As I note elsewhere, the image of the eye evokes the figure of the seer. Here, the blackness of the papoose's eyes also suggests reality—suggests the mystery of wilderness, the landscape of God or the Great Spirit, untouched by civilization. For a moment, Laura becomes one with that blackness and knows this is what she wants, although she cannot explain what it is. This experience is the culmination of her education on the prairie, and she never forgets it; she will refer to it again and again in the later books.

Thirteen

Joseph Campbell identifies the number thirteen as "the number of trans-formation and rebirth . . . of getting out of the bounds of twelve into the transcendent" (*Power*, 25). *Little House in the Big Woods* tells of one year in 13 chapters; *Little House on the Prairie* tells of one year in 26 chapters, which can be divided into two parts each 13 chapters long. Perhaps this structure reflects Wilder's desire not only to provide safety or predictabil-ity, but also to suggest the mystery and reverence with which she holds these two places in her memory. In any case, these novels are visionary: they slip out of the bounds of everyday life and realistic fiction into the realm of myth. In *Little House on the Prairie*, Laura experiences oneness with the prairie, the wolves, and the papoose. She encounters the sacred.

Seasons

The seasons provide a circular structure—another source of symbol-ism. The novel begins and ends in spring, the time of beginnings, birth, and the return of vegetation; and it takes place mostly in summer, the season of youth, heavy work for a pioneer or farmer, and being out-doors. Fall—the season of maturity, harvest, and celebration—is very short in this novel; as is winter, the season of old age and death, end-ings, rest, and being indoors. Thus the seasons not only provide a cycle, with its reassurance of predictability; given Wilder's decision to emphasize spring and summer, they also emphasize beginnings and activity. In addition, as one completed cycle, they signify not a vicious circle but a sacred circle. Laura is released, as the number 13 suggests, to wonder and awe as she experiences wilderness as mystery, infinity, freedom, beauty, and truth—as the eternal.

Leaving the Second Little House

At the end of the novel, our attention turns again to a little house, as once again the Ingalls leave a house behind. This time, however, less attention is paid to the house (324–25) than to the loading of the cov-ered wagon (320–24). Again Laura personifies the house: "It did not seem to know they were going away" (324); and "The little log house . . . sat lonely in the stillness" (325). In the final pages of the novel, however, she celebrates the covered wagon as a home—a moving home in which "you never know what will happen next, nor where you'll be tomorrow" (327).

The Journey Again

Clearly, Laura has learned at some deep level to prefer the journey to the house, the wilderness to civilization, the unexpected and unknown to the predictable and safe, action to stillness. For her, risk is preferable to boredom, as we see in *On the Banks of Plum Creek,* where she hates the house in the ground as overly confining and is repeatedly tempted by dangers (such as swimming in the deep hole of Plum Creek when Pa has expressly forbidden it). Wide-open spaces, the sunlight and warmth of a summer day, movement, risk, many new things to look at, experiences that activate her imagination, moments of wonder—all of these come when she lets go of the little house and becomes one with the flow of life. So, of course, does danger.

So also does learning how to be prepared for danger and how to respond to it. I think this is the point of the "tenderfeet" incident in the last few pages of *Little House on the Prairie* (328–31). The tenderfeet are unprepared, with no chains for their horses and no dog for protection, and so they lose their horses and find themselves stranded in the middle of the prairie. Had the Ingallses not come along, they would surely have died there. The contrast between the two families is obvious. The Ingallses know better, as their successful year has proven. By now, Laura's security is not in place but in action. The closing song and dream, about wandering (335), reveal this, and it will also be revealed in the next two books. Laura still has much to understand about what she has learned on the Kansas prairie, as we see when she nearly drowns in the flooded Plum Creek. Primarily, she must discover that she dare not take risks when she is unprepared to deal with the consequences. Secondarily, she must recognize the importance of both sides of a duality. That learning will structure the next five books.

Balance

The style and structure of *Little House in the Big Woods* and *Little House on the Prairie*—and their relationship as balanced opposites—

convince me that, never elevating one part over another, Wilder values wholeness, union, and oneness. The series acknowledges that in life, there is often imbalance, confinement, limitation, apparent chaos, fear, suffering, and separation. Such unsought experiences, if they don't destroy us and we don't run away from them, prepare us for further experiences. One side of any pair of opposites may dominate for a while, but eventually the other side will ascend. In the entire circle of existence or life, we see that everything is a necessary part of the whole, existing in tension with its opposite and sometimes in balance. In such moments, the center and the circle are identical, and the oneness of reality becomes apparent.

The Mythic Journey in the Other Little House *Books*

I cannot talk about *Little House on the Prairie* without talking about its partner in the series, *Little House in the Big Woods,* and I cannot talk about any of the other books without talking about its partner.[14] *On the Banks of Plum Creek* balances *By the Shores of Silver Lake; Farmer Boy* balances *The Long Winter; Little Town on the Prairie* balances *These Happy Golden Years.*

A lack of center or circle—formlessness—characterizes *On the Banks of Plum Creek.* "Center" contracts to a dugout; "circle" expands to a swarm of grasshoppers; nothing is quite right. A moving center and a circle of prairie return in *By the Shores of Silver Lake.* Both books, as adventure stories, are full of action. But *On the Banks of Plum Creek* is chaotic, offering little freedom or transcendence, although Laura does learn a great deal about the need to be prepared with knowledge of how to live; it introduces Laura to the "vicious circle." By contrast, the flowing action of *By the Shores of Silver Lake* again frees her to envision reality as oneness and stillness, this time within. She commits herself to working so that Mary can go to a college for the blind, experiencing in the Reverend Mr. Alden's prayer a "quietness [that] was a cool and gentle rain falling on her. Everything was so simple now that she felt so cool and strong, and she would be glad to work hard and go without anything she wanted herself" (*BSSL,* 219).

The circle contracts as the Ingallses are reduced to very nearly nothing in *The Long Winter,* but it holds. The absence of almost everything except the circle of family and Almanzo (who reappears) balances the abundance in *Farmer Boy,* the second novel in the series. *Farmer Boy,* the story of Almanzo's childhood on a New York farm, contrasts with the story of Laura's childhood on the frontier.

Little Town on the Prairie, the next-to-the-last book in the series, echoes *Little House on the Prairie,* the second book about Laura. A circle of people replaces the circle of wilderness, and the focus shifts to civilization and Ma, away from nature and Pa. In *The Long Winter* Laura learns that nature can be overwhelming unless her own internal center is strong; similarly, in *Little Town on the Prairie,* she learns that people too can be overwhelming, when tempers, disrespect for others, or religious fervor gets out of control. She herself learns self-discipline. In her words, "I will have to make myself be good. This is what it means to be free" (*LTP*, 76).

Then in *These Happy Golden Years,* as her circle of people contracts during the week to the Brewsters' shanty or to her students in a one-room school, she expands this lesson, recognizing that she cannot control others. In Mrs. Brewster's anger at living in a claim shanty and in her own anger at her students, she sees ineffectual effort to change or manage people. She learns that she is able to teach her students effectively when she praises their accomplishments and tries to see things from their point of view. When she marries Almanzo—without a promise to obey but as his partner—and they go to live in the "Little Gray Home in the West," the circle is complete and ready for a new beginning.

A MYTHOLOGY FOR THE PLANET

It seems to me evident that the *Little House* books connect, rather than divide; that they emphasize the worth of everything, rather than exalt one thing over another; and that they celebrate oneness or union as they swing back and forth between the dualities of western Christianity. In their portrayal of wilderness as sacred, they resemble Native American mythologies. In their stress on partnership, they remind us of Abraham and the "chaos revolution." In their mindfulness and their interest in wholeness or oneness, they seem mystical, perhaps even Buddhist.

Finally, the *Little House* books are about how Laura and the reader are to live. They build up a picture of the person little Laura is to become. Often chaotic and undisciplined at first, but eventually self-disciplined and selfless, Laura is both her mother's and her father's daughter. Her parents nourish in her a basic trust in life, whereby she can experience oneness with people and nature, civilization and wilderness, and all the other supposed dualities. As a person, she balances and preserves what she has learned from her mother and her father. This is the subject of Chapter 6.

6

The Inner Journey: Laura's Development

Laura turns five in *Little House in the Big Woods* (97–98), which ends in autumn before her sixth birthday. *On the Banks of Plum Creek* begins in summer after her seventh birthday (7). Between the two, of course, lies the year of *Little House on the Prairie*, which must begin in the spring after Laura turns six and end in the spring after she turns seven. However, Laura's age is not mentioned in *Little House on the Prairie*. Given that her family moved to Kansas some time in 1869 and to Walnut Grove, Minnesota, in 1874, we know that Wilder's Kansas experience occurred some time between her second and seventh years.

Because of these discrepancies, we need to be careful about expecting Laura to have specific characteristics usually associated with six- and seven-year-olds. We might even expect to see the behavior of a two- to four-year-old. Moreover, Laura comes from a culture different from that of children living today, and experts agree that culture significantly affects development.[1] Thus Laura might not have any characteristics typical of today's children from two to four or from six to seven. On the other hand, she can be understood as we understand young children in general, in terms of their mythic thinking[2] and their need to accomplish certain developmental tasks.[3] We will find that, despite the difference in contexts, Laura engages in the major developmental task of five- to seven-year-olds: constructing a model of the world beyond their homes.[4]

Mythic Thinking

It seems serendipitous that Egan chooses the word "mythic" to describe the thinking of the young child, which he calls the "foundational layer of educated adult thinking" (35). As he notes, he might have used some other word (for example, "poetic" or "fantasy"). He chose "mythic" because of certain similarities between myths and the earliest form of human thinking: (1) The characteristics of both persist "into rationality at a fundamental level" (41). (2) Both rely on "narratives which provide intellectual security by making a totalized sense of the world and of experience" (41). (3) These "narratives of myth and children are commonly story-shaped" (41). (4) "Myth-users and children charge their environments with meaning and significance in a way not common for modern educated adults" (42). (5) "Prominent among the structural features of children's and myth-users' thinking is the use of certain kinds of classification, prominent among which is the use of binary opposites" (42). (6) "Techniques of thinking . . . rely on the resources available within oral cultures" (42–43).

With regard to point 1, in discussing the later books in the series, I show that the mythic thinking of the first books persists in Laura's development into a rational adult. Points 2 through 5 are clearly true of *Little House on the Prairie*. In Chapter 5, I suggest that the goal of *Little House on the Prairie* is the second characteristic—a vision of wholeness—especially in conjunction with *Little House in the Big Woods*. Regarding the third characteristic, in Chapter 4, I discuss the novel as "story-shaped"—with a clear beginning, middle, and end, completely reversing its hero's fortune at the end. I address the fourth characteristic primarily in Chapter 3, but discussions of symbolism in Chapter 4 and religious implications in Chapter 5 also explore how Laura charges her "environment with meaning and significance." Throughout this study, I emphasize the fifth characteristic, the novel's

reliance on binary opposites for organization. We see the sixth characteristic—its use of "techniques of thinking that rely on the resources
available within oral cultures"—in its traditional opening; its cyclical
structure; its reliance on oppositions, repetition, and balance; and its
apparently independent incidents, each chapter existing to some extent
as a story that could stand alone. In these ways, the novel reflects the
characteristics of oral literature such as fairy tales—characteristics
which make such stories easier to remember and deliver.

BOUNDARIES

As mythic thinkers, young children lack a clear sense of boundaries,
limits, or contexts. They tend to identify themselves with their world;
therefore, "oneness" or "wholeness" aptly describes their experience
of life. Egan identifies language as "the first disrupter of . . . intimate
participation in the natural world" (93) because, as I note in Chapter
5, it creates distance between the self ("I") and nature ("me"). What's
more, because of their sense of oneness, young children are "accus-
tomed to thinking of spiritual ideas in terms of material properties and
physical places" (Damon, 10).

   Thus Laura's identification with prairie and house, Pa and Ma,
Native Americans and settlers—all the binary opposites the book
uses—is characteristic of the mythic thinker. Because we see from her
point of view, the world portrayed always reflects her state of mind. At
some level, then, this book is simply a portrait of Laura as a young
child—of her component parts and potential conflicts. In the later
books, we will see her become increasingly the mediating space—the
chaos between—but here she contains all.

BINARY OPPOSITES

In "Emigrant Selves: Narrative Strategies in Three Women's
Autobiographies," an analysis of the *Little House* books, *Out of Africa*,
and *The Woman Warrior,* Sarah Gilead argues that "the use of polar-

ized pairs of concepts to structure the narrative and to generate its key metaphors and images . . . project[s] its autobiographical self. That self is psychologically conflicted along the lines of the polar concepts. The primary strategy of the work is to transform such conflicts into the map of an idealized self holding these opposites in equilibrium."[5] We see this idealized self in *Little House in the Big Woods* and in *Little House on the Prairie,* the first two books about Laura.

Here, too, "material properties or physical places" express the spiritual or the psychological. As Gilead points out, metaphors of open and enclosed space evoke this "idealized self":

> The open spaces represent the self in process, capable of imagina-
> tive and idiosyncratic responses to external and internal change,
> but threatened with instability and indeterminacy. This self may
> tentatively be termed the "pioneer" or "emigrant" self . . . and is
> the effective cause of the narrative. At the same time, an enclosed,
> socialized self, product of both social and narrative expectations,
> is the logical end of the narrative. (43)

In the first novel, the little house introduces and celebrates the "enclosed, socialized self" and, distantly, in Pa and the big woods, the "pioneer" self. In *Little House on the Prairie,* the prairie powerfully evokes Laura's first experience of the "pioneer" self, but the novel also recreates the "enclosed, socialized" self, as Pa builds another little house and Ma makes it a home. The series as a whole drives toward the triumph of the socialized self, expressed in its final image of the little gray house in the west.

Although Wilder movingly portrays each little house as snug, cozy, and safe, her images of wilderness power her narrative. In *Little House in the Big Woods,* images of wilderness are safely confined to Pa's stories and games; but in *Little House on the Prairie,* they break free of that confinement to become Laura's (and the reader's) experience, though always within limits. The window and the house separate her from the wolves. The house keeps her warm and dry when there is bad weather. Her parents, Soldat du Chêne, and Jack the dog stand between her and the Native Americans screaming for war. Wilder's autobiographical fiction gives the reader only vicarious wilderness, always safe because always enclosed and somewhat distant, but increasingly suspenseful. Paradoxically, what is framed and bounded makes it possible for Laura, and the reader, to experience what is unbounded and unframed. As the remaining books will show, without limits such as those imposed here (window, house, parents, heroic Native American, Jack the watchdog, and the book itself), wilderness would kill us. On the other hand, too many limits also create a kind of death. Only in the space between the pioneer self and the socialized self can Laura, and life, flourish. Increasingly, as the series progresses, that space shrinks. It finally exists mostly within Laura, except as Wilder—the writer and Laura's adult self—preserves it in these books about her childhood.

PSYCHOSOCIAL DEVELOPMENT: ERIKSON'S STAGES

I see *Little House in the Big Woods,* reinforced by the openness and attention to detail of *Little House on the Prairie,* as conveying Laura's achievement of Erik Erikson's first stage of human development—basic trust (rather than mistrust). Its image is the cozy, snug, safe little house. (According to Erikson, this stage is completed by 18 months.) The second novel about Laura, with its prairie image of freedom, gives us (by its end) Laura's achievement of Erikson's second stage: autonomy (rather than shame and self-doubt). As I point out in Chapters 4 and 5, with Pa as her mentor, she begins her own love affair with wilderness; by the end of this novel she prefers a moving house and a journey to the little house's permanence and stability. (Erikson holds that this stage, autonomy, is completed by age three.)

Here, too, as she follows Pa around; imitates him; Mr. Edwards, and the cowboys; and wishes secretly to be an "Indian child"—we see signs of the third stage: initiative and imagination (rather than guilt). A child supposedly achieves this around age five, but in the wilderness Laura knows very well that she must obey her parents at once and never break any of their rules. She emphasizes this in two incidents: when she sits up while crossing the flood-swollen creek and when she thinks about unchaining Jack, though her father has forbidden it. In both cases, disobedience would increase danger. Thus in this novel "initiative and imagination" take the form only of resistance to gender socialization—Laura's dangling sunbonnet and her brown face.

Erikson's third stage is actually more fully expressed in *On the Banks of Plum Creek,* where Laura's initiative and imagination lead her to risk getting into a flood-swollen creek and almost drowning; and to risk "flying" from haystacks, thereby ruining the livestock's food for winter. In *On the Banks of Plum Creek,* largely because she feels confined by house and farm, she more often dangerously tests her limits and feels guilty because she has disobeyed. Also, on the whole, she succeeds with many of her initiatives, often displaying great imagination; for example, when a blizzard threatens during Ma's and Pa's absence, she and Mary carry the entire woodpile into the house.

Industry (rather than inferiority), Erikson's fourth stage, is usually not begun until age five and not completed until age ten. But Laura already seems to be well into this stage in *Little House in the Big Woods:* she expects to work for the family's comfort and survival, fetching hickory chips for Pa in the first chapter so that he can smoke a deer he has killed, and helping Ma with the housework, in ways of which a four- to five-year-old is capable. As a six- to seven-year-old on the prairie, she fetches and carries for Pa throughout the building of the house and does the dishes, makes beds, sets the table, and watches the baby for Ma. In *On the Banks of Plum Creek,* she and Mary increasingly become Ma's partners on the farm and in the house, because Pa must go east to find work that pays. *Plum Creek* covers two and a half years, ending just before Laura's tenth birthday. Then three years pass, and the fourth stage is definitely completed when *By the Shores of Silver Lake* begins. Laura is then almost 13. Everyone but Pa and Laura has had scarlet fever, and Mary is blind. Jack dies, and Pa goes to DeSmet to begin working. Ma relies heavily on Laura. Although still longing for the freedom of the prairie, for riding fast horses, and for any other kind of vigorous motion, near the end of this novel she finds within herself the still, refreshing center that makes "her glad to work hard and go without anything she wanted herself, so that Mary could go to college" (*BSSL,* 219). The enclosed or socialized self, the center previously represented by the little house, is now internal.

Erikson's fifth stage, usually begun around age ten and completed in late adolescence, is identity (rather than role diffusion). Although Laura begins to assert her identity as an adult in *By the Shores of Silver Lake,* the last three books of the series focus on this stage and its resolution. In *The Long Winter*, she learns that she cannot control nature, but that she can do whatever is in her power to endure—even when it threatens her life, as it does during this winter of blizzard after blizzard and insufficient fuel or food. It is in this book that the Ingallses are most seriously threatened and harmed; and Laura understands fully that wilderness can and does destroy, and that only she can control her response to such threats. Here the pioneer self begins to be internalized—understood as her freedom to control herself.

Little Town on the Prairie introduces her to community: its pleasures, its dangers, and its importance to survival and growth. She works in town as a seamstress. At school, she makes close friends and meets an old enemy (Nellie Oleson from Plum Creek). Both at school and in church, she learns that emotion out of control (her anger at her teacher and at Nellie and the Reverend Mr. Brown's fiery passion during the revival) is another form of wilderness, of nature, or of "pioneer" self that can emerge quickly and become destructive. She helps Pa put up hay when they are on the claim; but in town, she enjoys a variety of social events, studies to be a teacher, and gives Almanzo, her future husband, permission to walk her home from church.

She is still sometimes a child, running and rolling on the prairie; and she still identifies more with the wilderness than with the town. Sometimes she also still identifies more with being male than with being female, but she is moving toward a consolidation of her identification with Pa and with Ma and the binary opposites they represent for her. She recognizes that Pa and Ma will soon stop telling her what to do, and she will have to make herself be good. In her words, "That's what it means to be free. It means you have to be good. . . . Then you have to keep the laws of God" (*LTP,* 76–77). Equating freedom with responsibility (rather than with rights), she transforms the pioneer self into the socialized self in one step. The book ends when, at age 15, as the school's top student and one of the star performers at the school exhibition, she earns the community's praise and her first teaching job.

The Inner Journey: Laura's Development

In *These Happy Golden Years,* she leaves home to teach and must survive in a little house pervaded by Mrs. Brewster's half-mad anger and despair at living in a claim shanty. She has already learned that only she can control herself. Now she learns that she cannot control anyone but herself—not Mrs. Brewster, not her students, and not Almanzo. She develops her relationship with Almanzo as his equal, accepts his proposal, marries him, and moves into her own home— "the little gray house in the west." She has internalized the values initially expressed in her portraits of little houses and wilderness. Her security and freedom exist within. They are part of her identity. Ma's steady, quiet persistent, self-sacrificing care, and Pa's love of journey, risk, wilderness, freedom, and independence, are now within Laura. The socialized self is evident externally in Laura's acceptance of— indeed, pleasure in—female clothing and fashion. The pioneer self survives in her refusal to wear corsets at night and in images of wild drives over the prairie behind the latest horses Almanzo is breaking. But both selves unite in a young woman whose self-confidence, refusal to obey anyone, insistence that she is anyone's equal, and commitment to the welfare of others express both her security and her freedom.

GENDER AND MORAL DEVELOPMENT

As Michael S. Pritchard argues in *On Becoming Responsible,* both caring and justice are necessary to moral development,[6] but typically we rear women to value caring and men to value justice, just as we urge women to seek security (connections) and men to seek freedom (separateness). Like most scholars interested in moral development,[7] Pritchard tries to combine Kohlberg's view of justice as the goal of moral development with Gilligan's view (in *In a Different Voice*) that women, as a result of socialization, take caring as their goal. It seems clear that, as Pritchard and others point out, caring is as important as justice, and that Kohlberg misunderstood and undervalued caring, probably as a result of his own socialization as a male. As I have suggested, caring becomes women's highest value because women experience relationships as a system of connections nurtured by caring.

Nancy Chodorow, a psychoanalyst, sees the female predilection for connection as rooted in girls' childhood experiences with their mothers. Deeply attached to, nurtured by, and identifying with their mothers, girls grow up having empathy for others and cherishing relationships. Conversely, boys, who must break their primary bonds with their mothers to identify with fathers, grow up feeling separate from, and in competition for, their mothers and other resources. They therefore need rules and regulations to ensure that justice—fairness and equity—will prevail.

Under patriarchy, justice has triumphed over caring. But many women and men today believe that caring is more important to the survival of our world. Feminists, especially, have argued that an ethic of caring rests on what Jean Baker Miller calls women's "greater recognition of the essential cooperative nature of human existence."[8] Stephen Trimble's "A Land of One's Own: Gender and Landscape" supports Miller; Trimble argues that only faith in connection—with each other and with nature—will save the environment and foster peace.[9] Julia T. Wood, in *Who Cares? Women, Care, and Culture,* also supports this contention, but she points out that women's caring in the past grew out of their subordinate social position, that it has always been defined as a private activity rather than a social issue, and that its costs for women (and also for other marginalized members of society) have been very high—for example, motivational displacement (from the self's motives to others' needs), compromised or undeveloped autonomy, and devalued and low status.[10] Wood argues that we must make caring a social issue, not a private issue. Miller, Trimble, and Wood seek a new mythology for the planet.

This discussion of men's and women's moral development serves to introduce the complexity of gender issues in *Little House on the Prairie* and the other *Little House* books. As I have already pointed out, the critics disagree about this. Lee praises Ma's increasing worth in Laura's eyes and welcomes Laura's socialization toward becoming like Ma, that is, quiet, steady, and caring. Segel honors Wilder's books for their questioning of "the pernicious doctrines of repressive gentility and racial superiority." Mowder celebrates the books for offering a different version of the American frontier story: Whereas the usual version portrays a solitary man (or a man and his male companion of color) venturing into the female wilderness and conquering it, Wilder's version is of "a physical and psychological ground domesticated by women" (18). Wilderness, according to Mowder, is masculine (as represented by Pa) and childish (as represented by Laura), and Ma domesticates and civilizes both. Mowder seems to be aligned with Lee and Gilead with Segel. Gilead laments the loss of wilderness at the end of the series and identifies Ma as the conservative force in the novel—"the reality principle itself, as defined by communal consensus" (46).

My own reading of Laura's moral development, stressing balance or equilibrium, includes both views. Their apparent opposition results from the complexity of Wilder's symbols. Nothing represents an absolute good—neither wilderness nor civilization, Pa nor Ma, child nor adult, freedom nor security, the prairie nor the little house or town, vigorous motion nor stillness, the pleasure principle nor the reality principle, justice nor caring. Wilder's good is relative: some blend of the two. Her ideal is a balance of the two. Her final image of the little gray house in the west is a balance; the little gray house, symbolizing Laura's socialized self, is in equilibrium with the west, a symbol of her pioneer self.

As an account of Laura's increasing consciousness, the novels "record a series of endings and losses: childhood's end, the taming of the West, the expulsion of the Native Americans from their lands, the disappearance of the buffalo and other wild animals, Pa's relinquishing his desire to keep pioneering forever" (Gilead, 49). But they also record a series of beginnings and gains: the beginning of adulthood; Laura's learning self-control; the joy, activity, and variety of pioneer town life; the time and effort saved by technology (farm machinery and the railroad); the safety of a settled landscape; and Pa's commitment to put down roots for his family's welfare. To say that these beginnings and gains balance the endings and losses would be to miss the authenticity and power of Wilder's self-portrait. Growing up is by its very nature a series of losses. These are real losses that Laura must grieve for, accept, and integrate. The gains, to some extent compensating for the losses, assist in this integration. But as the writer of these books, Wilder never minimizes all that is now gone. The books are a powerful elegy for her childhood.

GROWING UP FEMALE ON THE FRONTIER

According to Anne MacLeod, such an elegy is characteristic of women's autobiographies and autobiographical fiction in the nineteenth century.[11] What MacLeod calls "the Caddie Woodlawn syndrome" controls this writing. She explains, "Many American families allowed their little girls to live nearly as unfettered and vigorous an outdoor life as their brothers. Country children, in particular, roamed their world without much restriction" (100). We might consider Laura's childhood freedom and love of physical activity and the out-of-doors as unusual, but this is not borne out by the evidence. Furthermore, Laura—like Caddie—discovers at puberty that the price of her freedom "is accepting greater restrictions on her freedom and higher standards for her behavior" (98) than are required of men. Consequently, Wilder and "many American women could and did look back to their childhood years as a period of physical and psychic freedom unmatched by anything in their later life" (100).

Writing of women who grew up as pioneers, Carol Fairbanks calls them "the second wave" (157–81) and contrasts them with women like Ma who became pioneers as adults and whom she calls the "first wave" (76–117). Fairbanks discusses the rise of feminism and realism in women who wrote out of their own experience of growing up on the frontier. These women, she points out, are not only more independent than women of the first wave, but are also the heroes of the stories about themselves (167). They suffer neither isolation nor loneliness to the same extent as their mothers, responding positively to the space and beauty of the prairie (171–72). Clearly, Laura is a woman of the second wave, choosing not town but a farm on the prairie and insisting on being her husband's partner on the farm.

THE DEVELOPMENT OF A WRITER

Wilder embodies her love for her childhood in the first two books about her childhood, but in the second—*Little House on the Prairie*—lament for the loss of wilderness is already apparent. Speaking of women's feelings about the sharp contrast between their lives as children and adults, MacLeod says:

> Women's resentment of their lot must have surfaced in dozens of ways we can only guess at. It surely emerged . . . in children's books, and often, paradoxically enough, in the very stories which were written with conscious intent to perpetuate the conventional ideal. Responses ranging from outrage to something like mourning run just under the surface of books utterly conventional in their openly asserted attitudes. (117)

As a farm woman, Laura avoids some of the physical restrictions placed on women of her day. From her pioneer childhood, she preserves her love of the outdoors, her determination to work alongside her husband on the farm, and her personal freedom, expressed in her refusal to obey anyone, including her husband. Nevertheless, we experience a tremendous sense of loss when she accepts the confining dress for women of the time, takes jobs sewing and teaching when she hates both, and sacrifices herself for Mary and her family. This loss is what Julia Wood calls the cost of caring.

However much we might regret Wilder's own concessions to the physical and psychological restrictions of the female role, it must be evident that they established the conflict between pioneer self and socialized self which is the foundation of the *Little House* books, expressed mythically in the balance of the two selves in the first two novels and increasingly realistically in the remainder of the series. As Gilead puts it, the series "powerfully resurrects the emigrant/child-self," and "to bring what is lost into the frames of literary art is, if not to save it from extinction, to resist in some small measure consenting to its loss" (49). I would add that Wilder also preserves the enclosed-socialized self.

As she takes Mary's place as Ma's primary helper, Laura comes to understand and respect Ma, learning to see her not just as Pa's opposite but as a complex person. Ma models caring for Laura—both its benefits and its costs. If Ma's focus on the safety, comfort, and happiness of her family makes her unnecessarily fearful and critical of Native Americans and of the frontier, it also makes her dedicated to creating a home wherever she is and to doing whatever that takes, no matter how much she may detest doing it. She would rather not go west, where school, church, and community are not available; where wild animals and men may injure or kill one of her family; and where tremendous physical effort and time must be put into wresting a living from the earth, with no guarantee that it is even possible. But she goes, as hopeful as her husband that they will improve their lot. In the first two books, she never complains and always defers to Pa. But increasingly, as Laura pays more attention to her, she emerges as a strong voice in the family. Settled in De Smet, she will not move. She insists that the girls get an education, that the family go to church, and that the girls experience civilization.

Although Pa remains a romantic figure throughout the series, the careful reader begins to see that there is some childishness in his love of wilderness—a constant longing for what might be, as opposed to what is; a refusal to put down deep roots; and an unwillingness to accept limits and adult responsibility. By the end of the last book, he too emerges as a complex figure—although he is still Laura's favorite parent and the one with whom she identifies more. His vision of life becomes Laura's: a journey into the unknown, the wilderness; an encounter with transforming experiences; a sense of oneness; a renewed journey. Pa has taught her to imagine, to take the long view that releases one from boundaries and liberates one into the possibilities of the imagination and the experience of oneness. But the caring—the motivation to pay attention, especially to the small details that make survival possible and life beautiful—she gets from Ma. She needed both to write the *Little House* books.

Finally, when she becomes Mary's eyes, Laura is also an author in training. Throughout the series, Laura is looking, and the eye functions as a symbol of the imagination. She watches both Ma and Pa perform as pioneers; she looks at the circle of prairie, wolves, and fire and at the line of Native Americans passing the little house; and she sees into all the life inhabiting prairie and little house. Like the black eyes of the papoose, Laura becomes the eye of the imagination, seeing into the mystery of a circle of violets to describe them as a fairy ring, only to have Mary, her mother's daughter, reject the imagined for the "real," or at least the pragmatic.

Between the poles of Ma and Pa and all that they represent, Laura constantly attempts to balance the real and the imagined, the details of daily life and the dreams of the imagination, civilization and wilderness, stillness and activity, security and freedom, the familiar and the unknown, limits and transcendence, caring and justice. Pressed too far, either pole negates the good of the other and can become overwhelming (like the long winter) or excessively confining (like a corset). Only in rare glimpses do the books disclose that it can be fatal to be stuck too long at either extreme—for example, when the crowd of rough railroad men in *By the Shores of Silver Lake* get drunk and kill the paymaster in a nearby camp. Life oscillates between these two poles, with occasional moments of balance; this is the rhythm of the *Little House* series and the wisdom at the heart of Laura Ingalls Wilder.

7

The Historical Journey: American Myth

THE ROMANTIC WILDERNESS: PRIMITIVISM

Roderick Nash contends that "wilderness was the basic ingredient of American civilization" (xi). He defines the idea of wilderness as "the unknown, the disordered, the uncontrolled" (xi) and notes that "ancient biases against the wild are deeply rooted in human psychology" (xi). This is also the opinion of Frederick Turner in *Beyond Geography: The Western Spirit against the Wilderness*[1] and of Yi-Fu Tuan in *Landscapes of Fear.*[2] Nash hypothesizes that the beginning of civilization, usually associated with the rise of herding and agriculture and the end of nomadism, resulted in the idea of wilderness, the one idea being necessary for the creation of the other. Before civilization existed, then, there must have been only the idea of differing environments, either open and spacious or dark and dense (Nash, xiii–xvi).

Given humanity's long-standing fear of wilderness and hostility toward it, Nash recognizes that "appreciation of wilderness is nothing less than revolutionary" (xi). He points out that the first positive feelings emerged not among the pioneers settling this country, but in the safe, settled cities of Europe. He calls this concept the "romantic wilderness" (Nash, chap. 3) and associates it with European romanticism of the late eighteenth and early nineteenth centuries. The concept can actually be traced to the enlightenment; with the rise and appreciation of scientific explanations of nature's laws, the deist idea of God and the aesthetic idea of the sublime in nature both emerged. Gradually, the city, civilization, and artifacts became the enemy, as the romantics increasingly valued "the strange, remote, solitary, and mysterious" (Nash, 47)—that is, the wilderness, nature, and the natural. Primitivism posited that humans are innately good and close to God and are corrupted by civilization. With this understanding, writers elevated all that was primitive—the child, the Native American, and the wilderness. Most of us would recognize primitivism as central to Rousseau's thinking.

Wilder's Romantic Wilderness

Primitivism is also obviously central to Wilder's presentation of Laura, Pa, the little house, the wilderness, and the Native Americans in *Little House on the Prairie*. Her distance from her childhood experiences in Kansas and her lack of direct memories affect her view of the wilderness. She knew, of course, that the Ingallses survived their Kansas experience, and her books suggest that this experience was central to the person she became. She refers to it many times in the later books, where it becomes a kind of touchstone or center by which she evaluates her later experiences.

The people, places, things, and events of this novel are somehow bigger than life. In Laura's young eyes, Pa as a pioneer and Soldat du Chêne as a "noble savage"[3] are heroes; the prairie is the lawn of God (when it is not a hell inhabited by demons—wolves, panthers, and Native Americans—or fire); the little house occupies the center of a magic circle that keeps the Ingallses safe; and she herself is, in desire and somewhat in fact, a free, wild, brown Native American girl. Thus, not only does her point of view tend to offer either an ideal or a demonic world; it also idealizes the primitive—elevating her, Pa, the log cabin, and sometimes the prairie and the Native Americans.

THE CONFLICT BETWEEN WILDERNESS AND CIVILIZATION

Whereas Nash traces the historical evolution of our idea of wilderness in general, especially in history, Leo Marx's *The Machine in the Garden* focuses on literature. Marx begins with the English Renaissance, in particular with Shakespeare's *The Tempest*. In his second chapter, "Shakespeare's American Fable," he shows that the discovery of what Henry Nash Smith called "virgin land" profoundly affected Shakespeare and other Elizabethans. He contends that the plot of *The Tempest,* centered on the "hero's struggle with raw nature on the one hand and the corruption within his own civilization on the other" (35), prefigures America's primary conflict and, structured as a "redemptive journey away from society," "the design of the classic American fables" (69).

Wilderness versus Civilization in Wilder

As we have seen, the conflict between wilderness and civilization motivates the design of *Little House on the Prairie*. It is civilization that Pa wants to escape; it is wilderness that he desires. Indeed, the evidence suggests that we are to consider him a wild man—whose hair always stands up and who feels at home only in nature, free of other settlers. The Ingallses go on a journey into the wilderness, away from society. Introducing Laura to wilderness, this journey will make it impossible for her ever to be fully satisfied with civilization or ever to value security over freedom. All of the later books reveal that this experience of the prairie evoked a love and respect for all wilderness that would be at the core of the woman and writer she became. Out of this center, furthermore, she was eventually to create a redemptive experience for her readers.

THE CONFLICT BETWEEN NATURE AND ART: PRIMITIVISM, PROGRESSIVISM, AND PASTORALISM

As Marx points out, Shakespeare expands the conflict between wilderness and civilization so that it becomes a conflict between nature and art. Marx sees this broader conflict as universal and traces the complexity with which Shakespeare treats it. Within the scheme of *The Tempest,* Marx finds, Shakespeare presents three responses to nature. (1) The first response essentially celebrates nature as good and civilization as bad. (2) The second response sees nature as needing to be transformed by art if human good is to prevail. (3) The third response sees all art as part of nature and calls for a proper balance between art and nature. Marx identifies the first view as primitivism and the second as progressivism (though he also describes both as "simplistic pastoralism"). The third view, the main theme of *The Tempest,* Marx calls "complex pastoralism." He compares complex pastoralism to the cycle of psychic experience in which we move from "routine waking consciousness" to sleep and dreams, to "the act of love, perhaps even death where the race renews itself if only in making room for the newborn" (70), and back to waking consciousness. In life and in complex pastoralism, Marx insists, the experience of balance is always temporary, always what Frost identified as the function of poetry—"a momentary stay against confusion." *The Machine in the Garden* explores the ways in which the American wilderness generated all three responses in literature, arguing that the best works are characterized by complex pastoralism.

Primitivism, Progressivism, and Pastoralism *in* Little House on the Prairie

In *Little House on the Prairie,* nothing suggests that the experience of balance is anything but temporary. The novel ends with the Ingallses' journey out of the wilderness. Pa's comment as they take their last look at the little house suggests why—artistically—the experience had to end: "It's a great country, Caroline. . . . But there will be wild Indians and wolves here for many a long day" (325). Although the Ingallses have survived for one year, this wilderness is a genuinely dangerous place that would eventually have destroyed them—unless they destroyed it. In any case, only by leaving can they offer us a balanced experience, a momentary stay against confusion. In the remaining *Little House* books, a dialectic rhythm between civilization and wilder-

One pioneer family alters the prairie.

ness (waking and dreaming) is also evident, but never again does it create the balance of opposites achieved in *Little House in the Big Woods* and *Little House on the Prairie*.

Essentially, then, *Little House on the Prairie* takes what Marx identifies as Shakespeare's third view of nature and art: a temporary balance. But it also presents both primitivism (chiefly through Laura's perceptions) and progressivism (in the views of some of the white settlers and in the behavior of all of them).

Progressivism is apparent as we see one family transforming the wilderness: building a house and stable near an old trail used by the Osage, digging a well, acquiring a cow, killing wild animals for food, and plowing up wild prairie for fields and a garden. We also hear that there are other white settlers engaged in these activities. In Mrs. Scott's criticism of Native Americans for "never do[ing] anything with this country" (211), we hear the pioneers' belief in progress, defined as farming the land for human purposes rather than letting nature take its course. Obviously, the Ingallses would not be in Kansas if they were not looking for a better life than they had in the Big Woods. In Pa's words after his first day's hunting, "there's everything we want here. We can live like kings!" (50). References to the day they will begin living like kings become a refrain in the novel. Although we respond immediately to the image of the wilderness as abundance and ease (a primitivist theme), we cannot ignore that a king not only enjoys nature's bounty but also owns and rules the land.

THE AMERICAN FRONTIER: PROGRESSIVISM AND TECHNOLOGY

From the beginning, Nash demonstrates, American pioneers responded to the frontier—the wilderness—as progressivists. They considered wilderness "as much a barrier to progress, prosperity, and power as it was to godliness" (Nash, 40). In other words, it was bad, in both secular and sacred terms. In Robin Winks's words, "The Frontier itself encapsulates the opposition of the good against the bad, the west against the east, the simple against the sophisticated, America against all others, and now [the 1960s] nostalgia against change" (8).

The myth of the frontier was articulated in 1893 by Frederick Jackson Turner as the "frontier thesis" of American history. In this theory, the western United States, until it was settled, provided psychological and physical resources that shaped American character and history. As much a process as a geographic area, the frontier, according to Billington, functioned as a safety valve for undesirables such as the poor, the discontented, and the oppressed (1958, 13–20). According to Turner, it was a way out no matter what one's reasons for departure might be; it stood for unlimited resources and offered hope that, with effort, people could improve their lot in life. Thus the pioneer exploited the wilderness, killing off wild animals like the buffalo, displacing or murdering Native Americans, chopping down forests, and plowing up land without any thought of conservation. The frontier of myth resulted in traits which are supposed to be characteristically American—optimism, individualism, mobility, materialism, wastefulness, and nationalism.

In their drive for progress, the pioneers welcomed and quickly became dependent on technology—another presumably outstanding characteristic of Americans.

As Marx understands progressivism, the machine—technology—is its chief tool and symbol. In our classic literature, the machine (for example, in the form of a locomotive in *Walden,* a textile mill in *Moby-Dick,* or a steamboat in *Huckleberry Finn*) often breaks in on a tranquil setting and disrupts it. The imagery is of a "female landscape" violated by "crude, masculine aggressiveness" (29). Marx argues that technology as much as wilderness shaped the American mind, and few would disagree. Indeed, technology—farm machinery, and especially the railroad—hastened the settlement of the immense wilderness, whose vastness called for inventions that would save time, provide comfort, and bring riches. Our pursuit and glorification of technology still thrive today, despite our awareness of the damage it has done to the earth and its inhabitants—pollution of the air and water, depletion of the ozone layer, elimination of many species, accumulation of weapons capable of eliminating human life, and a frantic, stressful pace of living. Some observers, like Bill McKibben, would say that our pursuit of perfection through technology has led to "the end of nature." Nash suggests that in the late twentieth century, even our passion for wilderness, requiring its careful management so that we do not love it to death, in effect eliminates what we desire to preserve.

Wilder's American Frontier: Progressivism and Technology in the Little House *Books*

When Wilder sat down to write her books, in the 1930s, she was fully aware of the myth of the frontier, and fully aware that the frontier was gone. She saw her childhood as a record that the frontier had once existed, and as a symbol of its meaning in the history of the United States. Although she would probably have disagreed with Roosevelt and his associates, she may also have been aware that they were arguing that "extension of government control over the economy . . . was necessary to provide the security and opportunity formerly provided by cheap land" (Billington, 1958, 42). As Billington shows, by the 1930s it was widely believed throughout the United States that the frontier had functioned to determine our national history and to define our national identity.

Wilder is less concerned in *Little House on the Prairie* with celebrating progress than she is in several of the other *Little House* books, yet we still find her commitment to it in this third book, as we would expect in any story about the frontier and pioneers. Here, however, the technology is simply that required for survival: gun, hammer, ax, shovel, and traps. The plow left behind when the Ingallses leave is perhaps the most advanced tool present.

In many of the other books, new machines are evident and are often praised in terms such as Pa uses about the threshing machine in *Little House in the Big Woods*. In a chapter called "The Wonderful Machine," he says, "That machine's a wonderful invention! . . . Other folks can stick to old-fashioned ways if they want to, but I'm all for progress. It's a great age we're living in" (*LHBW*, 227–28). The advance of technology—in particular, the building of the railroad—is a major theme in *On the Shores of Silver Lake*. Again the machine is praised, though this time in Laura's voice rather than Pa's. Chapters 3, 4, 5, and 10 are about, respectively, riding on a train, ending the journey, a railroad camp, and an afternoon watching grading in preparation for the laying of track. A near-repetition of the sentence at the end of *Little House on the Prairie* ("You never know what will happen next, nor where you'll be tomorrow, when you are traveling in a covered wagon") conveys Laura's excitement: "You never knew what might happen to you on a train" (*BSSL*, 16). More directly, we have her thoughts about her trip on the train: "She knew now what Pa meant when he spoke of the wonderful times they were living in. There never had been such wonders in the whole history of the world, Pa said. Now in one morning, they had actually traveled a whole week's journey [by wagon], and Laura had seen the Iron Horse turn around, to go back the whole way in one afternoon" (30). The speed and energy that amaze her in this episode also characterize the homesteaders' arrival and the building of the town.

At the end of *By the Shores of Silver Lake*, the family is living in town, and Laura hates it (149–54). In *Little Town on the Prairie*, she describes it as "a sore on the beautiful, wild prairie" (49). But this novel and *These Happy Golden Years* do celebrate civilization, and so (implicitly) does *The Long Winter*. In *The Long Winter*, it is obvious that for the Ingallses, surviving the many blizzards depends on their living in town. In *Little Town on the Prairie,* Laura works in town, goes to school and church, and attends a sociable, literaries, a New England supper, and a birthday party. She learns to "like living in town better than . . . [she] ever thought she would" (261). In *These Happy Golden Years,* isolated in the Brewster shanty and at the school, Laura especially learns to value her home and town. Returning on the weekends at first, and for good when her contract ends, she relishes her social life, education, church, and courtship. These books focus on the importance of community.

NATURE AS EDEN

McKibben laments that we have lost or eliminated nature—whatever is not human, is not made by humans, is not controllable by humans, and is often thought of as God. This is reminiscent of a very different literary response to the American wilderness: seeing it as a new Eden, the garden of God; and seeing the American hero—male, of course—as a new Adam.[4]

This hero, often guided by a Native American or an African American, retreats from a stifling, distorted, corrupt civilization (often identified with the female) into a pristine wilderness. (Interestingly, this wilderness is also often identified with the female.) James Fenimore Cooper's Natty Bumppo; Nathaniel Hawthorne's young Goodman Brown; Herman Melville's Ishmael; Thoreau, Emerson, and Whitman, in their journals and poetry; and Mark Twain's Huck Finn are only a few examples.

As we've seen, Nash calls this the "romantic wilderness" and believes it came to dominate American thinking as the wilderness disappeared; and it is this aesthetic response to wilderness that Marx calls "primitivism."

Wilder's Prairie as Eden

Mowder is correct in saying that Wilder associates wilderness with men (mostly Pa and Almanzo, but also several other pioneers and some

Native Americans) and children (Laura). Civilization is identified more with females in the first books, if we exclude Laura. In the later books, though, both Pa and Laura clearly enjoy the pleasures of civilization—for example, literaries and school. Beginning in *The Long Winter,* Pa is a leader in the community. The movement of the series, then, is not away from civilization into wilderness but, for Laura and Pa, toward the taming of the wild and the triumph of the civilized, internally and externally.

Nevertheless, it is the wilderness that inspires and animates Wilder's writing. Wilderness furnishes the occasions for great joy and deep sorrow in her books. We have seen this in *Little House on the Prairie.* First, we see it in Laura's joy when she plays on the prairie and in all those moments when she feels at one with the wild—when the stars sing and dance with Pa's fiddle, when the wolves encircle the house, when the nightingale sings with Pa's fiddle, when the sun rises and everything wakes up on the prairie, and when she locks eyes with the papoose. Second, we see it in her sorrow when the Native Americans leave the prairie.

This theme of Laura's joy and sorrow over the wilderness continues in *On the Banks of Plum Creek,* where her most intense joy is always in vigorous activity outside and her lament is for the lost prairie. Here there is less wilderness, and nature is more often destructive than beneficent. A creek nearly drowns her, grasshoppers destroy two wheat crops, summers are too hot and dry, Laura wishes she "was an Indian and didn't have to wear clothes" (219), and the winters bring blizzards.

In *By the Shores of Silver Lake,* the family returns to the prairie, and Laura is overjoyed. She tells us she prefers riding in the wagon to the train because "the wagon went slowly, so there was time to see everything. And they could talk comfortably together" (37). Laura delights in taking wild rides across the prairie on ponies, in walking on the prairie, in living on the claim, in taking care of the cows, and in certain fascinating "wild" people, such as cousin Lena, the railroad men, and Big Jerry. But by now there is also Laura's lament for the buffalo: "Laura had never seen a buffalo, and Pa said it was not likely that she would ever see one. Only a little while before the vast herds of thousands had grazed over this country. They had been the Indians' cattle, and white men had slaughtered them all" (61–62). Near the end of the book, Pa can find nothing to bring home for dinner and tells his family, "Looks like hunting's going to be slim around here from now on" (245). The last scene in the book combines Laura's love of the wild and her lament over it:

> The whole great plain of the earth was shadowy. There was hardly a wind, but the air moved and whispered to itself in the grasses. Laura almost knew what it said. Lonely and wild and eternal were land and water and sky and the air blowing.
> "The buffalo are gone," Laura thought. "And now we're homesteaders." (285)

In *The Long Winter,* wilderness is once again an enemy, burying the little town in blizzards for seven months. But the wild things by their behavior and an old Native American man, through a message—"*Heap* big snow, many moons" (62; he holds up seven fingers)—attempt to warn the town; and Pa takes notice and moves in from the claim. Actually, dependence on technology is as much the enemy as nature in *The Long Winter.* The lack of trees makes the townspeople dependent on the railroad for both food and fuel; and lack of food and fuel when the blizzards stop all the trains threatens their lives. Until the homesteaders get established, they are totally dependent on the railroad for supplies, and prices are high because the railroad must be paid the carrying cost. In addition, in *These Happy Golden Years,* at least distantly, we hear criticism of reliance on the new farm machinery. In Pa's words:

> "This giving a mortgage on everything he owns, to buy a two-hundred-dollar machine, and paying ten per cent interest on the debt, will ruin a man. . . . Let these brash young fellows go in debt for machinery and break up all their land. I'm going to let the grass keep on growing, and raise cattle." (197–98)

Whether Wilder intended this or not, then, the books clearly show that technology is as much a bane as a boon. Once a new machine exists and people begin to depend on it, no one can compete without it;

but then the cost of farming increases, requiring increased production. Successful farming is no longer possible unless one starts with the necessary resources—and that is highly unlikely for a homesteader.

In the last three books, the Ingallses live more in town than on the prairie. When they are on the claim, they struggle with needleweed and blackbirds, losing their crop of oats and corn two years in a row. Laura begins to face the reality that although the prairie "looks so beautiful and gentle," it seems as though "we have to fight it all the time" (*LTP*, 89). Still, it is not so clear that she accepts Ma's view that "this earthly life's a battle. . . . It always has been so, and it always will be" (*LTP*, 89). When Pa says one day, "I would like to go West. . . . A fellow doesn't have room to breathe here any more," Laura's reaction is significant:

> Laura knew how he felt for she saw the look in his blue eye as he gazed over the rolling prairie westward from the open door where he stood. He must stay in a settled country for the sake of them all, just as she must teach school again, though she did so hate to be shut into a schoolroom. (*HGY*, 138–39)

As much as these books are about love of family and friends, they are also about loss—of childhood, wild animals, Native Americans, wandering and exploring, vigorous outdoor work, wilderness, unrestricted freedom, a historical period, and a way of life. No matter how positive Wilder is about the march of progress, she always remembers fondly all that is gone and grieves for it. The undercurrent running throughout the *Little House* books—surely named, as most things are, to honor the victor—is a lament for wilderness.

THE AMERICAN HERO AS INNOCENT

Primitivism exists side by side with progressivism in much of American literature, often in direct conflict, especially during the nineteenth century. Much of the ambivalence, the rich ambiguity, of our greatest literature arises out of this conflict. Is the wilderness evil or good? Is civilization evil or good? Is technology evil or good? Are human beings innately evil or good? Is innocence preferable to experience? We have already noted the American hero as a new Adam; the hero as innocent is a related theme.

In *Love and Death in the American Novel,* Leslie Fiedler criticizes American literature for immaturity: its refusal to allow its heroes to grow up, its denial of racism and genocide, and its avoidance or fear of mature, sexual women. The house, a symbol of the hero's self or heart (for example, Hawthorne's *The House of the Seven Gables* and Poe's "The Fall of the House of Usher"), also symbolizes the distortion and destruction created by such immaturity. But Chase, Lewis, and Porte claim that heroes in American literature reveal, ironically, that innocence is both ideal and demonic. These heroes respond to the world with energy, grace, sweetness, openness, and creativity but also—in their rejection of imperfection—with egocentrism, arrogance, and destructiveness. They serve as an excellent measure of civilization's failures, especially of human alienation as the "things" of civilization gain in importance and human beings are increasingly cut off from nature. In Marx's words, these heroes rebel against "the increasing repression of instinctual drives made necessary by a more and more complicated technological order" (178).

Wilder's Characters: Innocence and Experience

In many ways, the *Little House* books reflect primitivism. Their hero—Laura—is an innocent, especially in the early books. Throughout the series, she rebels against "the increasing repression of instinctual drives." Although this rebellion lessens as Laura grows up, it still functions as criticism of the social norms of the adults who surround her. From Laura's point of view, we see that Mr. and Mrs. Scott's opinion of Native Americans results from a complete failure to look at the situation from another point of view, that Ma's fear and hatred of Native Americans is somewhat irrational, and that Pa and the other white settlers refuse to confront their mistreatment of Native Americans. We also see that a rigid gender role for women on the frontier is clearly inappropriate—indeed, that the expectations for women are crippling, both emotionally (denying them equal participation in family decisions) and physically (especially, forcing them to wear corsets). Then, too, we see that it is unjust to expect children to behave in ways that adults are unable or unwilling to model, and that relying on technology can be harmful.

But Laura's viewpoint also criticizes primitivism. It reveals that lack of social norms is even more destructive than "repression of instinctual drives." In *The Long Winter,* when Loftus attempts to charge the starving townspeople an exorbitant price for the wheat that Almanzo and Cap risk their lives for, we see the greed and communal irrresponsibility that were often evident in frontier capitalism. *Little Town on the Prairie* reveals that the frontier attracted many rough, lawless men, even killers; encouraged men to abandon the morality, rules, and order of civilization; and totally demoralized some women. The rough language of the men in Tracy; the man who rides up to the Ingallses on their trip to Silver Lake, intending them harm; the gang of railroad workers who nearly bushwhack Pa when they think they have been underpaid and intend to hang Big Jerry because they merely suspect him of being a horse thief; the claim jumper who kills a rightful owner—these are all examples of the failure of uncivilized men to curb their desires for the sake of community. Mrs. Brewster's wild anger and threats express her despair over her isolated, uncivilized life on the frontier. Laura's uncontrolled anger leads her to slap Mary (*LHBW*), to lead Nellie Oleson to a spot in the creek where Laura knows leeches will stick to Nellie's legs (*OBPC*), and to encourage the children to disrupt Miss Wilder's classroom (*LTP*). Wilder describes Pa's and Laura's constant desire to go farther west explicitly as against the best interests of the family, and implicitly as selfish and irresponsible.

Clearly, Laura's innocence functions like the innocence of heroes in much American literature—criticizing the rigidity of civilization but also recognizing the egocentrism, arrogance, and destructiveness of the innocent. As a character, Laura is every bit as appealing as any other hero in American literature, because of her energy, her enthusiasm, her spontaneous empathy with the underdog or the injured, her sense of fairness, her imagination, and her responsiveness to beauty, nobility, and grandeur. Her point of view, furthermore, has the rich ambiguity and ambivalence typical of our national fiction. Primitivism vies with progressivism, each revealing the limits of the other. Unlimited desire for wilderness as Eden or for wilderness transformed into a land of plenty is destructive.

But there are profound differences between Laura's story and the stories of many other American heroes. For one thing, Laura does grow up. Second, her story does not deny racism or even genocide; it always suggests the complexity—and the dark side—of the frontier response to Native Americans. Third, Ma is a mature, sexual woman, as are many other mothers in the novels.

With regard to this third difference—sexuality—it is true that nothing is shown beyond a woman's sitting on her husband's knee or hugging and kissing him, and even these are rare. Still, Pa does not leave his wife and family except when necessary; and if it is not actually pictured as a mature sexual union, Ma and Pa's relationship is evidence of mature love between a man and a woman. Pa, like the typical hero of American fiction, longs for wilderness, perhaps because he is unable to settle down and commit himself to a place; but he stays in De Smet because of his commitment to Ma and the girls. Furthermore, in a time when men made the decisions for the family, we see Ma playing an increasing role in decisions, especially about whether or not to move again. As Laura grows to understand Ma, we see that Pa always consults Ma and that what Ma says about what the girls may or may not do, and about family decisions that may affect the girls, prevails. In fact, we could say many of the same things about Laura and Almanzo's courtship. Laura places them on equal footing when she tells Almanzo not to pick her up at Brewster School if he expects her to be indebted to him, but only if he does so of his own free will. She is always his equal in their decisions and refuses to promise to obey him as part of her marriage vow. Although they don't often speak their feelings or show much physical affection, their love is evident in their enjoyment of being together and in their missing one another when they are apart.

One other point might be made about mature sexuality in Wilder's works: Before the late twentieth century, little more than Wilder shows of sexual relationships was shown in any children's books. This seems justifiable if one assumes that children are not interested in or ready to handle literature portraying adult sexuality, and in any case it is easily explained, given the prevailing social attitudes toward sexuality before midcentury. There was considerable reluctance to portray sexual relations openly even in literature for adults—and surely this accounts, at least in part, for the fact that "the great works of American fiction are notoriously at home in the children's section of the library" (Fiedler, xviii).

Laura's growing up, the recognition of racism, and the presence of mature sexual women, then, are significant differences between the *Little House* books and other classic American literature. Clearly, though, the most profound difference is that the hero of the *Little House* series is a girl. Considering the gender stereotypes of the time and the titles of many of the books, we expect a domestic tale; and, in addition to the adventure and wonder of pioneering, that is what we get. Although Laura is a tomboy before she reaches puberty, this was typical behavior for some girls of her time and place, as Anne MacLeod has shown. Gradually, she also learns to keep house, care for children, cook, and sew. As she grows up, we see her engaging in activities expected of women, including cultural events and schoolteaching. The last two books, about her courtship and marriage, are typical closing events in a domestic tale. Although Wilder intended primarily to show that her early life "represented a whole period of American history" (*LHS*, 217), her speech at the book fair in Detroit also tells us that she conceived of the series as an eight-volume novel of Laura's and Almanzo's youth and courtship, ending "happily (as all good novels should) when Laura of the *Little Houses* and Almanzo of *Farmer Boy* were married" (*LHS*, 220).

As noted above, in American literature the house is often a symbol of the hero. In a domestic tale, the house is always a setting and often reflects the personality of the woman or women living there. Ma does her best to make each little house an attractive home that will, in little ways, reflect the civilization left behind, just as she tries to educate her daughters to behave like ladies. Almost all of these little houses—a log cabin, a dugout, a claim shanty—are "wild" outside, like Laura herself, surrounded by wilderness. But all of them are clean, cared for, appealing, sturdy, cheerful, and (with the obvious exception of the dugout) full of light. Thus they reveal Ma's character and, indirectly, Pa's feeling for her. Laura's miserable experience in the Brewster shanty allows her, and us, to appreciate Ma's and Pa's graces as homemakers and parents. Each little house provides emotional and physical security—love—in the midst of wilderness. It never totally represses the wild, but it serves as a refuge and a center of stability when nature, internal or external, threatens to overwhelm Laura.

Ma and Pa model for their children how to live in a family and in a community. In the first books, because Laura is too little to experience much beyond her home, she knows only the family—a caring, interesting group of people who work hard and yet have fun together, telling stories, making music, playing games, and celebrating special events. In the attention and respect they give one another, we see their deep love, even when there is conflict and especially when there is loss. We see the same attention and respect given to neighbors. Cooperative ventures are common. As much as Laura's parents stress obedience when she is young and on the frontier, they also stress cooperation and mutuality. And as she matures, they increasingly treat her as an adult whose decisions are to be respected.

THE HERO AND THE SEARCH FOR NATIONAL IDENTITY

Daniel Hoffman argues persuasively that "the core of American experience has been a radical search for identity" (353), and that our literature, typically about an innocent's journey of self-discovery, reflects this search, defining our culture in terms of the innocent's discoveries. On this journey, the innocent hero encounters "characters representing the contending forces in his own psyche or the alternative commitments of belief, value, and action available to him" (357). "In his uncompromised rebellion . . . [he] declares his independence from family, from social class, from church and God, from history" (357). Hoffman sees the crucial American experience as rebellion against limits and imperfections. Not surprisingly, then, our literary ideal is Eden—a dream of oneness with virgin nature. This dream is symbolized evocatively in images of dear friends at one with the natural world—for example, Natty Bumppo and Native Americans alone in the pristine forest,

Ishmael and Queequeg at sea, or Huck and Jim floating down the Mississippi on a raft.

Marx, by contrast, suggests that in our best stories, innocence, as a result of experience, arrives at self-knowledge, that is, knowledge of human limitations and of nature's ambiguity and mystery. Such stories show that fusion with nature can be only temporary, literary, imaginative, or intuitive; otherwise, fusion results in death. Seas and rivers may drown—and wild animals, wild men, and nature may kill—the innocent. In order to live, to have food, to build shelter, and to protect ourselves, we must destroy nature. Life feeds on death. Thus to some extent, physical separateness from the "all" is a condition of survival. Separateness is perhaps even a definition of life as opposed to death, which returns the separate to oneness. Marx points out that the pastoral dream of oneness with nature ignores the fact that decay, destruction, and death are natural—a fact which motivates the "thrust of Western man for ultimate knowledge and power" (293).

These two views of nature represent, of course, primitivism and progressivism respectively; and both views seem to me motivated by the same goal—a desire to avoid or deny the reality that each individual consciousness is a brief spark in the great dialectical flow of existence between energy and matter. Each view fails to look at the whole. Primitivism focuses on oneness or "allness," the "childlike self, intoxicated by thoughts of innocent love" (Marx, 305), and ignores the threat to existence posed by wilderness—in oneself, in other people, and in other parts of nature. Progressivism encourages "ruthless, adult aggressiveness" (Marx, 305), seeking to eliminate or change all of nature that inhibits human life and to secure all that gives pleasure. Its goal is perfection. Focusing on outer threats to human existence, it ignores our potential for self-destruction and our limited understanding of the implications of our technology and our manipulation or elimination of nature.

In any case, it is abundantly clear that the primitivist dream of oneness with wilderness has found, in Marx's words, "no defense" (353) against the progressivist dream of power, since progressivism has been armed with increasingly sophisticated technology. In our best literature, Marx says, "ambiguity is the attribute of a physical universe that matches the contradiction at the heart of a culture that would deify the Nature it is engaged in plundering" (301).

National Identity in the Little House *Books*

Wilder's books are about Laura's search for identity, and they define our culture in terms of her discoveries. As we have already seen, we can read the characters as parts of her psyche or (in Hoffman's terms) as "alternative commitments of belief, value, and action available" to her. Although Laura does rebel—for instance, she prefers greater freedom and time outdoors than her gender role prescribes—her rebellion is not uncompromising. She defines herself by means of her family, social class, church, and history. She functions as their critic and their representative, both criticizing and holding primitivist and progressivist concepts of nature. Although she is aware of their constraints, she put on the apparel of an adult woman and takes up a teaching career for the sake of her family. Although she refuses to give up her love of the wild entirely (in the last book, this refusal is symbolized by her sleigh and buggy rides with Almanzo behind unbroken horses), she does accept limits. She chooses Ma's way—love and commitment to those one loves—even though that often entails doing what she dislikes and accepting what restricts her freedom. The family and the community take precedence over the individual. Furthermore, although Laura never ceases to love the land, she comes to realize that wresting a living from it, in her daughter Rose's words, "wears out human lives year by year" (*LHS,* 12).

Laura stands midway between Pa and Ma, sharing Pa's ambivalent, ambiguous relationship with the land and Ma's commitment to family, education, religion, and community—to civilization. Perhaps because she was a pioneer *girl,* Laura tells more than one story. She tells the story of the American pioneer as innocent and sinless in a garden of Eden but at the same time destructive, wasteful, greedy, and aggressive; and she also tells a new story about love, commitment, and limits. I suggest that this is a story seldom told in our literature—and that it is, in a sense, a female story.

This is also, notably, a story about making do with what you have, of recycling everything: For example, clothes worn in *Little*

House in the Big Woods become curtains in later novels; blackbirds shot to protect the oats and corn in *These Happy Golden Years* are cooked and eaten. A pronounced refrain in this series is "no great loss without some small gain." Nothing is wasted—except when they leave a little house behind. Pa's hunting reflects this attitude. He never shoots what they cannot eat, unless animals threaten their lives, and the series as a whole deplores the white settlers' wholesale destruction of the wilderness.[5]

Although it may be unintentional, the ethic that Pa and Ma model is "sustainability."[6] This means taking only what they need to live; finding their happiness primarily in relationships, with others and with the wilderness; and valuing only a few things—things made special by the attention they receive from their owners and by the scarcity of luxuries. This can perhaps be seen as an aspect of Marx's complex pastoralism; it is the kind of balance evident in Thoreau's *Walden* and in much of our greatest literature. But this approach to life has (like primitivism) been no match for progressivism. That is what Wilder may have meant to imply when Pa refuses, or is unable, to buy large farm machinery; and we know, of course, how many family farms fail when corporations buy up the land and use modern technology to farm it.

Finally, Laura's story—her search for identity—is about mutuality, balanced relationships between people. Mutuality becomes a model of caring, a standard for judging people's behavior on the frontier. It is, obviously, absent from the white settlers' relationship with the Native Americans. But it is equally obviously present in Laura's family, in Pa and Ma's relationship, and in Almanzo and Laura's relationship.

As is noted in Chapter 6, mutuality as an ideal has survived among women. It is privatized and thereby deprived of political power, and it too has been no match for progressivism. Many observers today, however, see mutuality, or caring—along with sustainability—as our hope for the future. John Cobb and Herbert Daly argue, for example, that if it becomes a social and political goal—not only a private ideal—we will be able to live happier, less destructive, and more just lives.[7]

The American Hero as Seer and Artist

Hawthorne was the first American writer to use an artist as the protagonist in many of his works (Lewis, 118–26; Porte, 138–51). Today, the artist, or seer, as hero is common in American literature. Such a hero may not be specifically identified as an artist but always has an aesthetic consciousness or sensibility: seeing nature and art, wilderness and civilization fully, and responding intensely and imaginatively. Stories with artist-heroes are characterized by heightened perception—and often by irony, when innocent characters present a more complex view of experience than they themselves apparently understand.

Charles Feidelson believes that American writers' interest in the writer as hero grew out of their own struggle with language, a struggle that has preoccupied Americans since the early days of the country. Controversies over the meaning of words plagued the Puritans, for example. Their most acceptable solutions, like those of later American writers, relied on a "symbolic 'language of paradox'" (Feidelson, 94–98). Obsession with relationships between thought, feeling, object, and word led early Americans to distinguish between knowledge from words and knowledge from experience. They preferred knowledge from experience, believing that the senses and intuition may grasp as unity what thought and language can present only as duality (98–101). The artistic temperament, then, as understood by our writers, is highly attuned to the senses and intuition. Feidelson's main point is that American writers found symbols better than abstract language for conveying "knowledge by experience," and that, besides the American landscape itself, the artist is one of their principal symbols.

Laura as Seer and Artist

As I note at the end of Chapter 6, Laura—like many heroes of American literature and children's literature—has an artist's temperament.[8] She functions very much like other artist-seer characters: She sees more than she understands, and she responds intensely and imaginatively. She also struggles with language, swinging between Mary's and Ma's preference for the literal and Pa's preference—and her own—for the imaginative. Her solution, too, is to convey "knowledge from experience"[9] by means of symbols, as we have seen throughout this study.

Wilder's own primary symbol is Laura, the writer-to-be. Wilder's desire in writing these books was to preserve her experience as a "pioneer girl." But as she wrote, at some level she must have been aware that her hero—herself as a child—would grow up to write about her experience. This is evident in a conversation between Mary and Laura in *These Happy Golden Years*. "I am planning to write a book some day," Mary says. Then she laughs and adds: "But I planned to teach school, and you are doing that for me, so maybe you will write the book" (136). Laura hoots at the idea, although it immediately interests her enough that she asks Mary what her book would be about. Laura's reaction is in character; all through the series she has struggled against anything that would keep her indoors but has often discovered that once there, she enjoys herself. Wilder here consciously lays the groundwork for her eventual decision to preserve her treasured memories of what she loved and lost.

In a way, every page of her books lays this groundwork, if less deliberately. Major symbols evolve out of Laura's perception of her response and other characters' responses to some reality—to a little house or to the prairie, for example. Everything in the books thus serves to characterize Laura as her identity evolves, and the series records the formation of a writer.

In Conclusion

Because of the nature of Laura's experience, the *Little House* books speak richly, and ambiguously, about many things: the American frontier, pioneers, our attraction to pantheistic mysticism,[10] our national and spiritual identity. They evoke what we were, what we had, and what many of us have lost—childhood; wilderness; a special period of our history; a native population and its cultures; awe and wonder in the presence of mystery; the pioneers' knowledge of how to live in a wilderness; recognition of cooperation and community as essential to survival, identity, and happiness; naive and ardent commitment to ideals such as freedom, independence, equality, and progress—and, on the other hand, a certain blindness to our self-contradictions and our destructiveness. In the *Little House* books, Wilder returns all this and more to us. As long as the books are read, nothing is altogether lost.

Wilder's gift of her own experiences as a child allows us to perceive and evaluate our nation's childhood: to open our eyes to its contradictions and possibilities. It may also let us appreciate her repeated implication that "little" may be enough; and that if we can accept what is little, "big" need not overwhelm or destroy us or tempt us to overwhelm and destroy, but can transport us into a momentary connection with mystery—with everything that is and might be. The little house is enough for Laura, even as she experiences the vastness and mystery of the prairie. Her moments of oneness are full of a deep joy that seems essentially religious.

In the context of the other *Little House* books, of Laura's growing up, and of our nation's history and spirit, *Little House on the Prairie* sings of balance, limits, and caring for the "other." To balance opposites is to assert equality—equality of people, places, objects, and events. To recognize limits is to see the other as a source of identity, existence, and joy. To care is to pay attention to the other: who or what it is, what it needs, and what its true potential may be. Balance, limits, and caring: All three are important to those of us who want to redirect our country toward (in Cobb and Daly's words) "community, the environment, and a sustainable future." I would like to think that, as much as *Little House on the Prairie* grieves over loss, it also presents a model of how to live—a model that may secure the future I would want for my grandchildren's grandchildren.

Appendix: Approaches to Teaching
Little House on the Prairie

CONTENT

The organization of this book suggests much of what I believe students should be taught. In Chapters 1 and 2, we look at background material that deepens our understanding and appreciation of the novel: its fame throughout the world, especially as a television series; some biographical information about Wilder as author and Lane as editor; some history of the time when the book takes place and the time when it was written; some information about the other *Little House* books; and some attention to the ways in which the contexts of contemporary readers will affect their understanding of the book. Chapter 2 provides an overview of the book's critical reception and of many of the ideas explored in later chapters. In Chapter 3, we consider the detail with which Wilder presents places, animals, people, objects, and events. In Chapter 4, we look at the novel's structure (plot) and symbols. In Chapter 5, we examine some of its spiritual themes; in Chapter 6, some of its psychological themes; in Chapter 7, some of its sociopolitical themes.

ACTIVITIES

Only the imagination limits the number and kind of activities that might be used to teach this book. Several resources offer a variety of these.[1] Some relate exclusively to *Little House on the Prairie*. Others include activities for some or all of the *Little House* books.

Standard features of these resources are lists of vocabulary to be studied and specific comprehension and review questions. Some resources offer suggestions for bulletin boards (Hacket, Rozakis). Most include maps with the *Little House* sites identified and various mapping assignments. In a few there are book summaries for all of the books (Hacket, Rozakis). One (Troy and Green) teaches students how to make "attribute webs" of characters, places, and things; it also asks students to construct story maps of single events, leading to a map of the whole novel, and to try to predict what will happen next, explaining the basis for their predictions. Taken together, these resources offer students many suggestions for research topics: the prairie, the Homestead Act, wolves, Native Americans in Kansas (or in any of the states where the Ingallses lived), the pioneer lifestyle (including clothing, necessary possessions, food, building materials, farming practices, and games), and many others. One resource asks students to prepare annotated bibliographies of some *Little House* books (Porta-Center). All these resources offer some biography of Wilder as a pioneer and writer or ask the students to find out about her. Some give writing assignments on what it means to move, what a home is, how it feels to lose a pet (or something else as important as the Ingallses' dog Jack), what the illustrations add to the books, how the novel uses sounds, why a hearth is important, why neighbors were necessary for a pioneer, what Pa's many sayings mean, why sharing is important, what differences there are between camping then and now (or school then and now, or Christmas then and now), and many others. Many also give ideas for art projects such as a mural of one event, a drawing of the high prairie camp or of Jack's return, and making paper dolls and clothes for a pioneer family. In addition, there are suggestions for dramatizations, games (including cat's cradle and bean porridge hot), newspapers, newscasting, and oral reports. Instructions are given for making butter, pancakes, or corn meal mush. Troy and Green and Niles, Popp, and Throop recommend that students learn some of the songs Pa plays, for example, "Old Dan Tucker." Other ideas include creating models of the log cabin or town and taking field trips to prairie restorations, pioneer sites, or *Little House* sites.

Note: There are mistakes in some of these materials for teachers. For example, two incorrectly identify the setting as Oklahoma rather than Kansas; and most display little understanding of the Osage and sometimes resort to stereotypes about Native Americans that I would wish to correct when using them with students.

READING ALOUD

With elementary students, I like to read these books aloud. Teachers can read the first three books to first-graders. My own informal polling of teachers and college students indicates that the series, if read as a whole, is most commonly read to third- and fourth-graders. My preference would be to follow Wilder's plan: she intended the books for increasingly older children. Thus the first three would be read to first- or second-graders, the next two to second- or third-graders, and the last three to third- or fourth-graders.

My experience suggests that some children, beginning as early as second grade, will not want to wait until I read again and will finish the novel I am reading aloud on their own and often go on to the next one. This is not a problem unless the entire class is doing it—and usually not even then, because all people (even teachers!) love to be read to.

I preface my first reading aloud with a few remarks about how everyone loves being read to. With older students, I cite a few statistics[2] about advantages for nonreaders, and tell a few stories from my own experience of reading to children and of being read to by "books on tape." Like many other adults, I love listening to books while driving, walking, exercising, and cleaning. If students are skilled readers or there is some reason that the teacher cannot read aloud, this can of course be limited or even eliminated. I strongly urge, though, that teachers read aloud frequently in literature classrooms at all levels.

The following sections consider several specific aspects of teaching about this book.

LITERARY AND HISTORICAL CONTEXTS

Fame

Before beginning to study this novel, teachers should address its fame. Asking the students how many of them have heard of *Little House on the Prairie* or any of the other *Little House* books is a good way to begin. Many will know only the television program, and those who know about this book may not have read it and may not have heard about the other ones. I always ask how many know about the television program and have discovered over the years that although nearly everyone has some knowledge of it, often (even in college classes) more than 50 percent have not read the books. After hearing the students' responses, I offer a few facts about sales, prizes, and the general consensus that the *Little House* books—and especially *Little House on the Prairie*—are classics. I ask students to keep this critical reputation in mind as we study the books.

Television Show

I find it useful to conduct a discussion of the television show as preparation for reading the book, suggesting that readers keep the show in mind and note differences as they read. If students have not seen the show, I point out that it is being aired on TBS and ask them to watch a few episodes. It would also be easy to videotape two or three episodes for use in the classroom, though I have never needed to do so. After reading the book and comparing it with the show, one might also show the videotape *Little House on the Prairie—Premiere Movie.*[3] Alternatively, this video could be used instead of the episodes currently being shown, as a basis for comparison. This is a two-hour televised version of the book, first shown at the beginning of the series in 1974. Since it is on the whole much closer to the book than the television show, it affords an opportunity for making finer discriminations between book and dramatization.

Appendix

Students will notice that some episodes are missing, such as building the doors, roofing the cabin, building a fireplace, laying the floor, digging a well, visiting the Native American camp, having "fever 'n' ague," Pa's going to town a second time, the panther's screaming in the night, and the long line of Native Americans riding away. Teachers might ask students why these episodes were left out, as a preface to discussing the different demands of different media: especially time constraints, but also the difficulty of maintaining interest when there is great detail or repetition. Also, the effects of different media differ, and students' ideas about these effects must be sought. The book offers more security, for example, a greater sense of time passing; the voice of an older, wiser Laura as narrator; a fuller impression of what life was like; and so forth. The televised version is more sentimental and melodramatic and faster-paced.

There are also additions to and changes in the televised version. From the beginning, Laura is excited rather than bored by the trip. We often share Pa's point of view rather than Laura's. We hear Pa's and Ma's conversation when they are alone; they are physically and verbally demonstrative to one another, as well as to other people, places, and events. Ma seems weak in her inability to help Pa lay the upper logs for the house (she shakes and collapses rather than being injured), and in her easy weeping; she seems fearful, in her crying out whenever there is danger; and she shows dislike in her ill-mannered treatment of Mr. Edwards and Soldat du Chêne. She is very stereotypical. Pa, as an unqualified hero, is also stereotypical. In every dangerous situation, he is more at risk than he ever is in the book; for example, when he jumps out of the wagon to guide the horses across the creek, he is swept under the wagon. Also, it is he who tells Laura that the stars are dancing and singing. Jack is not a brindle bulldog but a big, fluffy dog. The show also stereotypes the wolves that chase Pa: he is able to distract them with game he had shot, and they don't circle the house but pace back and forth before the fire at the door as if they might try to attack. Also Pa tells only Laura about the wolves' chasing him—so as not to frighten his wife! There is a blizzard at Christmas; this would be highly unlikely in southeastern Kansas, but it makes Mr. Edwards's going to Independence, crossing the creek, and trudging through the

131

snow in his long underwear very dramatic. We find stereotypes and inaccuracies in the Native Americans. Their full dress in buckskin is unrealistic, given the climate; their long hair was not worn by the Osage; and their behavior is always bad—with the one exception of Soldat du Chêne, who gives Laura a bear claw as an amulet. Some of the details are simplistic and even incredible. For example, can we really believe that a great Native American leader would, at a first meeting, give a white child anything as valuable as the amulet? Another incredible interaction occurs when Pa orders Laura never to disobey him, and she says that because she is not a baby, he should have told her why she was not to untie Jack. The remark is inappropriate, coming from someone of her age and time. Very little attention is paid to setting; the grass is not tall; and only one kind of small creature is named. Mr. and Mrs. Scott are not present; and soldiers, rather than the neighbors, tell Pa to move out. Finally, the Ingallses' leavetaking is sad, prolonged, and sentimental.

Still, for all its faults, this two-hour version of the *Little House on the Prairie* is by far more faithful to the book than the televised series is as a whole. In the televised series, the later episodes bear almost no resemblance to any of the books. The town of Walnut Grove, for example, becomes comically involved with incompetent criminals and fast food restaurants.

Biography

The teacher can simply provide information about the author, as appropriate for the age group, for the time available to be spent on the books, and for the book or books being taught. Students might also (or instead) read one or more of the biographies appropriate for their reading level.[4] Students may also wish to write to HarperCollins, 10 East 53d Street, New York, NY 10022-5299, for a biography (Porta-Center). They might also enjoy writing to one of the many sources of information about her life: Little House on the Prairie, Box 110, Independence, KS 67301; Laura Ingalls Wilder Home-Museum, Rt. 1, Box 24, Mansfield, MO 65704; Laura Ingalls Wilder Memorial Society, Box 344, De Smet, SD 57231; Laura

Appendix

Ingalls Wilder Memorial Society, Box 269, Pepin, WI 54759; Laura Ingalls Wilder Museum, Box 58, Walnut Grove, MN 56180; Laura Ingalls Wilder Park and Museum, Box 354, Burr Oak, IA 52131.

Information about the mother-daughter collaboration intrigues students in the late elementary grades and above. To give them some firsthand experience of what Rose may have added, a teacher can get a manuscript of any of the *Little House* books on microfilm from the University of Missouri, copy a page, and ask students to compare the manuscript and published versions to see what kind of editing occurred.[5] Another way of examining the respective roles of mother and daughter in the creation of the books is provided in the booklet put out by the Herbert Hoover Presidential Library. It contains letters written by Laura and Rose about Plum Creek and Silver Lake, along with questions designed to provoke understanding of the collaborative process (*LIW-RWL*).

History
Knowledge about Kansas from 1861 to the early 1870s will enrich students' understanding of this book. Although children's books about Kansas say little about this early period, there are some good books about pioneering and about the Osage and Cherokee.[6] Teachers will need to fill in some gaps, though, especially regarding gender roles.

Teachers also will need to introduce the concepts of manifest destiny and of the frontier. The frontier had closed by 1930, during the heart of a depression which many felt was caused by the absence of a frontier. This book offers some discussion of that period; of Rose Wilder Lane's rising anger over Roosevelt's social policies (and her mother's agreement); and of how the writing, the economy, and the mother's and daughter's uneasiness with government policies all came together. It also presents ideas about the effect of the frontier's closing and about the intersection of writer, editor, history, and the creation of the *Little House* books. Teachers can ask students to formulate their own opinions, using the books as evidence. Clearly, how much time should be spent on this depends on the maturity of the students.

The Series

At the very least, I provide summaries of the other *Little House* books, but I prefer to have the students read at least one other book in the series, preferably three or even more. I have assigned one of the books to each of eight groups and had each group report to the class about its book. However the teacher introduces the other books, students should note changes in Laura, the Ingallses' route over the country, changes in the environments, and differences in style and structure among the books.[7]

The Books Today

As I have already suggested by listing three writing assignments on comparisons between some aspect of "then" and "now," these books offer a multitude of opportunities for noting differences between life in the 1860s and 1870s and life today. I am particularly interested in tracing attitudes toward nature, toward Native Americans, and toward females from this period to ours. The ambivalence and ambiguity of our attitudes today can be found in *Little House on the Prairie,* although the later books enrich our understanding of how Wilder felt as an adult about Americans' attitude toward and treatment of nature, Native Americans, and females.

LITERARY ANALYSIS

Detail

The first level of understanding any work of literature is detail: its settings, characters, special objects, and events. The details provided about each create our image of it. Chapter 3 outlines what settings, characters, special objects, and events we find in this book. There are many ways in which students can compile the details creating each. An "attribute web" or drawing requires students to collect information about a specific character, setting, or thing. Story maps, construction projects (a miniature of the house or fireplace, for example), and murals focus on events. Review and comprehension questions can also involve compiling details about a person, place, thing, or action. Small groups might investigate different characters, settings, objects, or actions important to understanding the novel. Indeed, any number of strategies will help the students see how full of detail this novel is and how it functions to create evocative, concrete images.

Style and Structure

I like to begin any discussion of how a book is put together by asking students to identify one image that best recalls the book for them. They may describe this image in words or with a drawing. I then ask them to explain their choices. This leads us into a discussion of Laura, Pa, the little house, the prairie, the wolves, fire, Native Americans, and journeying. I then turn to comparisons of the book's beginning and ending, its chapter titles, the cycle of seasons and other circular images, the Native Americans' departure in a line, and the different implications of circular and linear images. Discussions of wild water and fire will lead to awareness of how threatening lack of order and lack of predictability can be. Next, I would direct students' attention to the 26 chapters and their obvious division into two parts of 13 chapters each, one about a house being built and the other about a house being threatened.

With regard to style, I ask students to point out opposites to me. We put a list on the board. Eventually we see that there is a continuum of places, persons, animals, and objects ranging from the wild to the civilized; and that abundant details, as well as comparisons evoked by oppositions, result in symbols—that is, evocative, concrete images. Finally, we spend some time with specific sentences (for example, those in the first two pages of the book). Individually or in groups, students describe the words and sentences in terms of concreteness or abstractness, simplicity or complexity, realism or fantasy, oppositions or comparisons. As a class, we then try to describe the pattern of a passage. For example, a passage may move back and forth between what is not understood but is imaginatively evocative and what is known and understood. This provides grounding for young readers.

Implications and Themes

Having acquired an understanding of contexts, details, oppositions, and circular or linear patterns, students are ready to talk about meanings—spiritual, psychological, and sociopolitical. Having discussed Wilder's attitude toward nature in the book, I would ask what the book says about religion or God or mystery. I would specifically want to know if the students think the book is Christian, and why or why not. Regarding Wilder's reverence for nature, I would ask how many of them feel the same way; if so, in what specific situations; if not, why not. This works best as a writing assignment. I would want them to think about who is in control in this novel—Pa, the Native Americans, God, or . . .? I would also want them to think about how much power and control any of us has, and what the novel says about power and control.

This would lead us into the novel's portrait of Laura and her limits and power as a child, a female, a European-American, and a pioneer. In other words, we can look at the novel as a psychological portrait of Laura. This lays a foundation for a discussion of its sociopolitical implications regarding age, sex, race, nature, and technology. As I have shown, *Little House on the Prairie* complexly embodies the American myth of the innocent living in freedom, equality, and harmony with humanity and nature, evoking all of its appeal for us, yet undermining any notion that there can ever be more than temporary, imperfect experiences of such balance. Evidence of ageism, sexism, and racism suggests an ethic of power over other people, rather than power with them—just as, in the other books, the use of technology to conquer the land suggests an ethic of progress, that is, of humanity in control of nature.

On the other hand, in *Little House on the Prairie* a balance is maintained. A parent needs control over children if the family is to survive in dangerous situations. For all of Ma's efforts to curb Laura's freedom and will, she models herself after Pa. Pa, although a pioneer and hunter, is usually very gentle and is as much a dreamer as a "doer." Opinions about Native Americans range from extreme racism to respect. Although relieved when the Native Americans stop drumming and yelling for war, the Ingallses are nevertheless saddened by their departure. The book thus masterfully captures the ambiguity, ambivalence, confusion, and contradictions of the American mind, which I would want students to see and understand.

Teachers would also want to show how the book is intriguing for what it might teach us about the value of "little" and "big." We are coming to recognize in the late twentieth century all of the losses entailed in hierarchical power and "bigness." When a group, an area, or an organization is huge, those at the top of the hierarchy cannot possibly know many of the people or much of the space about which they make decisions. The smaller the number of people and the area they occupy, the more likely it is that their interests, the well-being of nature, and the good of the whole will be met. It is difficult to harm or destroy people and places we know. We immediately see the effects of our bad decisions—and others do, too, and are likely to replace any leader who does not take good care of people and the environment. Small-group discussions or writing assignments begun in a group about the relative merits of "little" and "big" produce some interesting results. My experience suggests that students have generally learned by first grade that "big" is better than "little," and that this idea impairs their self-esteem. Challenging this idea always livens things up.

One family in one little house in the wilderness have more than enough, but they take only what they need. They alter the landscape, but they practice "sustainability." On the other hand are the settlers crowding onto Native American reserves, the other frontiersmen slaughtering the buffalo, and the United States government removing the Native Americans. In later books, the Ingallses sometimes don't have enough, but when they do, having enough is always sufficient to their happiness. It is not possessions but connections with people and the land that bring them joy. Things can be essential to their survival or to their sense of themselves as individuals, but people and places are what finally count. In the last two novels, community expands from one family and their few neighbors to a little town. Just as Laura learns from Ma that caring may require putting others before herself, she learns from her experiences in town the interdependence of all life. To be sure, it is the dream of abundance that motivates the pioneer to move farther west, but the *Little House* books demonstrate that it is the imaginative potential of the west rather than its material potential that moves Pa and Laura. They want to see more than they want to possess.

Even very young students can understand the difference between a Christmas dreamed about and a Christmas actually had. Things too often are less fun than we anticipate, especially when we have many things. Asking students to compare Laura's and Mary's Christmas with their own, in terms of both presents and happiness, will lead some students to see that the actual thing is not as important as delight in the special nature of a holiday and of gifts. Families spend the day together. Extra effort is expended to make or buy presents. Each gift embodies one person's love and regard for another. Good food and good cheer are hallmarks of a happy holiday. A comparison of Christmas then and now may thus lead the class into the subject of what makes a holiday happy. So may simply asking students to talk or write about what happiness is for them and for Laura, pointing out similarities and differences. It is important to have them share their ideas and, respectfully, challenge one another.

In these and other ways, students can begin to see the depth and complexity of meaning embodied in a simple little book written for children.

Notes and References

Preface

1. Alan Watts, *The Wisdom of Insecurity: A Message for an Age of Anxiety* (New York: Vintage Books, 1951); hereafter cited as Watts.

2. Throughout this book I cite references to the *Little House* books parenthetically by page numbers. Initials of the titles, as indicated in the Bibliography, are included when necessary.

3. For an extensive citation of works about American myth, see note 17 to Chapter 1.

4. Examples include conflict about gender, race, pioneering, good behavior for children, and nature.

5. For a description of this mother-daughter relationship, see William Holtz, *The Ghost in the Little House: A Life of Rose Wilder Lane* (Columbia: University of Missouri Press, 1993); hereafter cited as *Ghost*. Additional information will be provided in Chapter 2. See note 5 to that chapter.

Chapter 1

1. Cobbett Steinberg, *TV Facts* (New York: Facts on File, 1985), 77, 109, 233–301.

2. See John Dempsey, "Warner Home Video to Distribute 28 NBC-Produced TV Programs," *Variety* 304 (16 September 1981), 49–50; Colby Coates, "At A&E, Some of the Best New Shows Are the Old Shows," *Mediaweek* 2 (20 July 1992), 12; Matt Stump, "Turner in Talks to Acquire Hanna-Barbara," *Broadcasting* 121 (15 July 1991), 64; Stephen McClellan, "Soviets Say 'Da' to 'Dallas,'" *Broadcasting* 121 (15 July 1991), 23–24; Anthony Lejeune, "It's Not All *Brideshead Revisited*," *National Review* 41 (13 October 1989), 27–30; and Lisa Gubernick, "Why Rent When You Can Own?" *Forbes* 142 (5 September 1988), 38–39. Beginning in 1989, GoodTimes Home Video (401 5th Avenue, New York, NY 10016) made some

of the shows available in ten videos, each from one and a half to two hours long.

3.   In addition to the many books and articles written about Wilder (as listed in my selected bibliography as selected literary studies—a list that grows increasingly rapidly with the years), there are a variety of sequels and imitations, for example, the books published by Thomas Nelson; see William Griffin, "Harper, Nelson Face Off Again over Laura Ingalls Wilder," *Publishers Weekly* 239 (28 September 1992), 10.

4.   The show was so unfaithful to the books that many loyal readers were offended and attacked it. For examples, see David England, "Television and the English Teacher," *English Journal* 69 (November 1979), 99–102; Jake Newman, "Little House Divided," *Washington Post* (12–18 October 1980); "Little House on the Prairie," *Laura Ingalls Wilder Lore* 4, no. 2 (Fall-Winter 1978), 10; and Diane Roback, "Odds-On Favorites: Big Action at the Box Office Boosts Front Lists Sales," *Publishers Weekly* 240 (1 March 1993), 15–20.

5.   For examples, see Janet Spaeth, *Laura Ingalls Wilder* (Boston: Twayne, 1987), 91; hereafter cited as Spaeth; and Tim Brooks and Earle Marsh, *The Complete Directory to Prime Time Network TV Shows: 1946–Present,* 4th ed. (New York: Ballantine, 1988), 453–54.

6.   Throughout the book, Wilder generally uses the term "Indian." I will use the terms "Native American," "Osage," "Cherokee"—usages of the people to whom they refer.

7.   See Lane Diary, 1931–35, May-June Entries, LIW Series, Lane Papers, 19 May 1934 entry; Lane, talking about her work on the manuscript of the novel, refers to it as "High Prairie."

8.   I have previously written about Wilder's habit of uniting, not opposing, what are commonly thought of as dichotomies. See Wolf, "The Symbolic Center," "The Magic Circle," and "The *Little House* Books: A Personal Story."

9.   *Newsweek* (21 July 1980), 26.

10.   For a discussion of how postmodernism brings to the foreground the values of ambiguity, fragmentation, and openness, see David Harvey, *The Condition of Postmodernity: An Enquiry into the Origins of Cultural Change* (Oxford: Basil Blackwell, 1988); and Ihab Hassan, *The Postmodern Turn: Essays on Postmodern Theory and Culture* (Columbus: Ohio State University Press, 1987). Also helpful is Michel Foucault's *Power/Knowledge: Selected Interviews and Other Writings 1972–1977,* ed. Colin Gordon (New York: Pantheon, 1980). Foucault argues that any assertion of universal validity conceals reality: power is always one constituent of truth.

11.   See Hans-Georg Gadamer, *Truth and Method,* rev. ed., rev. and trans. Joel Weinsheimer and Donald Marshall (New York: Continuum, 1988);

Notes and References

E. D. Hirsch, *The Aims of Interpretation* (Chicago: University of Chicago Press, 1976); and Paul Ricoeur, *Interpretation Theory* (Fort Worth: Texas Christian University Press, 1976).

12. See Frank Kermode, *The Classic* (London: Faber and Faber, 1975); Perry Nodelman, ed., *Touchstones: Reflections on the Best in Children's Literature,* vol. 1 (West Lafayette, Ind.: ChLA Publishers, 1985), especially the introduction; and his *The Pleasures of Children's Literature* (New York: Longman, 1992), 107–8.

13. See my "Symbolic Center" for a detailed account of Laura's safety and security in the big woods.

14. I am grateful to William Holtz, "Closing the Circle: The American Optimism of Laura Ingalls Wilder," *Great Plains Quarterly* 4 (Spring 1984), 79–90, hereafter cited as "Closing," and to his *Ghost;* and to Spaeth, whose writing called the importance of this act to my attention. For detailed information about the act and its effects, see Ray Allen Billington, *Westward Expansion: A History of the American Frontier,* 4th ed. (New York: Macmillan, 1974), chap. 32; Robert V. Hine, *The American West: An Interpretive History* (Boston: Little, Brown, 1973); Henry Nash Smith, *Virgin Land: The American West as Symbol and Myth* (1950; reprint, New York: Vintage, 1957), chap. 15; and Walter Prescott Webb, *The Great Plains* (Boston: Houghton Mifflin, 1936), 398–413.

15. John Madson, *Where the Sky Began: Land of the Tallgrass Prairie* (San Francisco: Sierra Club Books, 1982); hereafter cited as Madson.

16. Holtz ("Closing") argues that Laura's family "failed . . . in history, [but] not in the world of Laura's books" (84). He points out that Pa was not able to keep his claim and that Laura, married to Almanzo, suffered every hardship Madson lists until finally the Wilders lose their land. *The First Four Years* details their struggle and suffering.

17. References in this note are hereafter cited by author's name. I use the term "myth" here in the broadest possible sense, including its social, political, and religious meanings as a guiding communal vision. My understanding of this concept has been formed by Northrop Frye, *The Anatomy of Criticism* (Princeton, N.J.: Princeton University Press, 1957); *Fables of Identity* (New York: Harcourt Brace, 1961); and, especially, *The Secular Scripture: A Study of the Structure of Romance* (Cambridge: Harvard University Press, 1976). Frye opposes myth and history and explores fiction as romance (close to myth) and as novel or realistic-mimetic fiction (close to history). In romance, he holds, characters are heroic and larger than life, whereas in the novel they are ordinary people. But the profound difference between romance and realistic fiction is their treatment of setting. As *The Secular Scripture* points out, romance requires stylized settings (both idyllic and demonic) for its structure.

In "The Magic Circle" and "The *Little House* Books," I explore Wilder's movement from romance toward realistic fiction through the eight novels, each intended for an increasingly older audience. *Little House on the Prairie,* relying heavily on stylized settings (like the first two novels), is very close to myth.

Myth is richly explored by many critics of American literature. See, for example, D. H. Lawrence, *Studies in Classic American Literature* (New York: Viking, 1951); Charles Feidelson, Jr., *Symbolism and American Literature* (Chicago: University of Chicago Press, 1953); R. W. B. Lewis, *The American Adam: Innocence, Tragedy, and Tradition in the Nineteenth Century* (Chicago: University of Chicago Press, 1955); Richard Chase, *The American Novel and Its Tradition* (Garden City, N.Y.: Doubleday Anchor, 1957); Leslie Fiedler, *Love and Death in the American Novel* (Cleveland, Ohio: Meridian, 1960); Ihab Hassan, *Radical Innocence: Studies in the Contemporary American Novel* (New York: Harper Colophon, 1961); Leo Marx, *The Machine in the Garden: Technology and the Pastoral Ideal* (New York: Oxford University Press, 1965); Daniel Hoffman, *Form and Fable in American Fiction* (New York: Oxford University Press, 1965); and Joel Porte, *The Romance in America* (Middletown, Conn.: Wesleyan University Press, 1969).

Historians also write of the frontier, the west, and the wilderness as important symbols of the American myth, beginning with Alexis de Tocqueville, *Democracy in America,* ed. Phillips Bradley, 2 vols. (New York: Viking, 1945); and *Journey to America,* trans. J. P. Mayer (New Haven, Conn.: Yale University Press, 1960). For other examples, see Webb (1936), Smith (1957), Hine (1973), Billington (1974). See also Billington, *The American Frontier* (Washington, D.C.: Service Center for Teachers of History, 1958), and his *Land of Savagery, Land of Promise* (New York: Norton, 1981), cited as Billington (1958) and Billington (1981). For wilderness as evil, see Carlton F. Culmsee, *Malign Nature and the Frontier* (Logan: Utah State University Press, 1959). For wilderness as a means of getting ahead financially, see Louis B. Wright, *The Dream of Prosperity in Colonial America* (New York: New York University Press, 1965). For wilderness as paradise, see Charles L. Sanford, *The Quest for Paradise* (Urbana: University of Illinois Press, 1961); and Howard Mumford Jones, *O Strange New World* (New York: Viking, 1965). Robin W. Winks, *The Myth of the American Frontier* (Leicester, England: Leicester University Press, 1971), discusses the effects of the frontier myth after the closing of the frontier in 1930.

Fundamental to our thinking about the frontier as essential to American myth is Frederick Jackson Turner, "The Significance of the Frontier in American History," in *The Frontier in American History* (1920; reprint, *The Turner Thesis Concerning the Role of the Frontier in American History,* rev. ed. [Boston: Heath, 1956]).

Like Winks, Roderick Nash traces the effects of the frontier myth into the late twentieth century, but he focuses on our attitude toward and policies about nature, rather than on the psychological, economical, or spiritual effects of the myth. His *Wilderness and the American Mind,* 3d ed. (New Haven, Conn.: Yale University Press, 1982) is a valuable resource.

Equally valuable are Robert N. Bellah, *The Broken Covenant: American Civil Religion in Time of Trial* (New York: Seabury, 1975); and Bellah's last two books with Richard Madsen, William M. Sullivan, Ann Swidler, and Steven M. Tipton, *Habits of the Heart: Individualism and Commitment in American Life* (New York: Harper and Row, 1985) and *The Good Society* (New York: Vintage, 1991). These works are more like Winks than Nash in their focus.

18. Quoted in William T. Anderson, ed., *A Little House Sampler: Laura Ingalls Wilder/Rose Wilder Lane* (Lincoln: University of Nebraska Press, 1988), 217; hereafter cited as *Sampler.*

19. See Donald Zochert, *Laura: The Life of Laura Ingalls Wilder* (New York: Avon, 1979), 22–51, for a reconstruction of the history on which *Little House on the Prairie* is based. Although Zochert does not cite sources for specific passages in his book, his preface notes that he relied heavily on the manuscript of "Pioneer Girl," which he calls "Laura's autobiographical memoir" (xii). Anyone familiar with the books and "Pioneer Girl" will see that he has, for the most part, retold the books, changing their story only when "Pioneer Girl" contradicted them. But he also altered events in accordance with his conversations with people listed in his preface, notably Irene V. Lichty, curator of the Laura Ingalls Wilder Home and Museum in Mansfield, Missouri; Margaret Clement of Independence, Kansas; and William T. Anderson of Davidson, Michigan, who has been a *Little House* scholar since boyhood. Zochert also examined the census of 1870 and read criticism of the *Little House* books. Finally, he describes the effort made by Laura, her daughter Rose, and the illustrator Garth Williams to find the location of *Little House on the Prairie* in Oklahoma, some 40 miles south of Independence (31, 33). See Williams's article in the special *Horn Book* issue on Wilder. I could not confirm from Lane's papers concerning the writing of her mother's books (especially Lane's diaries from 1926 to 1930 and from 1931 to 1935) that she and her mother ever took this trip to Oklahoma, although Lane did travel in Oklahoma (25–27 July 1933) to gather information for an article about wheat farming.

Noting Janet Spaeth's opinion that Zochert's book is "a bit too fanciful and vague with dates to be a solid scholarly tool" (Spaeth, 1987, 107), I have checked his work whenever I could. Zochert uses three dates to define the Ingallses' time in Kansas: 6 August 1869, 3 August 1870, and 30 May 1871. I could confirm only the second.

The first of these dates (6 August 1869), according to Zochert, is the day when Charles Ingalls signed power of attorney over to his father in Chariton County, Missouri. The trip to Kansas, we could logically assume, came shortly afterward. This assumption does seem probable, given that "the general influx of settlers into this part of the township was in the fall of 1869" (Thurman, 9; see note 20 below). But according to the Registrar of Deeds in Chariton County, there is no record that Charles Ingalls gave his father power of attorney, and Charles Ingalls did not sell his land in Missouri back to A. Johnson until 25 February 1870.

The second date (3 August 1870) is the day of Carrie's birth. This is recorded in the family Bible as occurring in Montgomery County, Kansas, so we know that they were still living in Kansas.

On the third date (30 May 1871), according to Zochert, Charles Ingalls revoked power of attorney in Durand, Wisconsin; this would suggest that the Ingallses left Kansas some time before. That Charles Ingalls had not filed a claim when his neighbors did, in June 1871, also supports Zochert's assertion that the family left Kansas in the spring of 1871. But Rita Conlin, Registrar of Deeds for Pepin County, says that to the best of her knowledge there is no record that Charles Ingalls revoked power of attorney. There is, however, a record of Zochert's coming to Durand, searching for records, and getting assistance from Emma Langlois, then the Registrar of Deeds. In a letter to her (4 May 1975), he sends a copy of a list of records supposedly available in her office. One book, Volume V of Miscellaneous Records, supposedly lists transactions regarding power of attorney since 1857. Rita Conlin showed me some old books she had that were not officially a part of her records. Two of them (arranged by property descriptions consisting of section, town, and range) listed all transactions with regard to a piece of property. Unfortunately, the Ingalls land (SW 1/4, Section 27, Township 24 North, Range 15 West) would have been recorded in a different volume. Perhaps Zochert had access to that volume. There was a fire in the courthouse in 1981, several years after Zochert did his research. Also, some of the old records are in an unlighted vault under the old courthouse—uncatalogued. In any case, whether or not there is or was a record of Ingalls's revoking power of attorney is a mystery I was unable to solve.

Zochert's biography is hereafter cited as Zochert.

20. See Evelyn Thurman, *The Ingalls-Wilder Homesites: A Diary of Visits 1972–83* (Bowling Green, Ky.: Lelley, 1982), 8–9; hereafter cited as Thurman. Margaret Gray Clement did the research on the location of the Ingallses' homesite in Montgomery County.

21. John Joseph Matthews, *The Osages: Children of the Middle Waters* (Norman: University of Oklahoma Press, 1961), 699; hereafter cited as Matthews.

22. For a map locating the 19 reservations in existence in 1846, see William Frank Zornow, *Kansas: A History of the Jayhawk State* (Norman: University of Oklahoma Press, 1957; reprint, 1971), 48; hereafter cited as Zornow.

23. See Ralph A. Barney, comp., *Laws Relating to the Osage Tribe of Indians, from May 18, 1824 to March 2, 1929* (Pawhuska, Okla.: Osage Printery, 1929; reprint, 1973). See also W. S. Fitzpatrick, comp., *Treaties and Laws of the Osage Nation as Passed to November 26, 1890* (Cedar Vale, Kans.: Press of the Cedar Vale Commercial, 1895; reprint, 1973). For background, see Matthews, 650–92; here we get the point of view of the Osage—a people steadily lied to and robbed as white settlers moved farther west into their dwindling reserve. For a strong condemnation of the portrayal of the Osage in *Little House on the Prairie*, see Dennis McAuliffe, Jr., *The Deaths of Sybil Bolton: An American History* (New York: Times Books, 1994), 110–12.

24. For a history of the Strip, beginning with the first treaty made about it and concluding with a description of the run on it by settlers in 1872, see William G. McLoughlin, *After the Trail of Tears: The Cherokees' Struggle for Sovereignty, 1839–1880* (Chapel Hill: University of North Carolina Press, 1993), 225–351.

25. Records of transactions for the deed for the Wisconsin property are available at the Registrar of Deeds for Pepin County in Durand, Wisconsin; for the deed for the Missouri property, at the Registrar of Deeds for Chariton County in Keytesville, Missouri.

26. She wrote about this in an undated letter to her daughter. See Lane's response, Laura Ingalls Wilder Series, Correspondence, 1908–ca. 1914, Lane Papers, Herbert Hoover Library, West Branch, Iowa. We have no other record of her attempts to confirm what she remembered their having told her.

27. Wilder to Martha Quiner Carpenter, 22 June 1925, Ingalls-Wilder Papers, Laura Ingalls Wilder Memorial Society, De Smet, S. Dak. See Aunt Martha's four letters in response, Laura Ingalls Wilder Series, Lane Papers.

28. See Zochert (44); Laura Ingalls Wilder Series, Lane Papers; and microfilm manuscripts of *Little House on the Prairie*, University of Missouri, Columbia. "Draft" is written on the backs of some letters, and the letter to the Kansas Historical Society is one of them. R. B. Selridge is my best translation of the signature to a letter dated 5 July 1933, included with two letters to Lane from Grant Foreman. These letters—along with a list of books, maps (one hand-drawn and one printed with a circle drawn around Independence and the area 40 miles south), some articles about the Native Americans of the area, and the typescripts of *Little House on the Prairie*—constitute the background material for the writing of the novel preserved in the Lane Papers, Laura Ingalls Wilder Series.

29. All the manuscripts of the *Little House* books are available on microfilm from the University of Missouri at Columbia.

30. The following are excellent studies of the Depression (hereafter cited by name of author): John Kenneth Galbraith, *The Great Crash, 1929* (Boston: Houghton Mifflin, 1988); John A. Garraty, *The Great Depression: An*

Inquiry into the Causes, Course, and Consequences of the Worldwide Depression of the Nineteen-Thirties as Seen by Contemporaries and in the Light of History (San Diego: Harcourt Brace Jovanovich, 1986); Robert S. McElvaine, *The Great Depression, 1929–1941* (New York: Times Books, 1984); Michael E. Parrish, *Anxious Decades: America in Prosperity and Depression, 1920–1941* (New York: Norton, 1992); and Harvey Swados, *The American Writer and the Great Depression* (Indianapolis, Ind.: Bobbs-Merrill, 1966).

31. William T. Anderson, "Laura Ingalls Wilder and Rose Wilder Lane: The Continuing Collaboration," *South Dakota History* 16 (1986), 89–143; hereafter cited as "The Continuing Collaboration."

32. For example, Holtz, 306–7; John Miller, *Laura Ingalls Wilder's Little Town: Where History and Literature Meet* (Lawrence: University Press of Kansas, 1994); and Anita Claire Fellman, "Laura Ingalls Wilder and Rose Wilder Lane: The Politics of a Mother-Daughter Relationship," *Signs* 15 (1990), 535–61. Hereafter, Miller and Fellman are cited by author's name.

33. See note 17 above.

Chapter 2

1. William T. Anderson, "The Literary Apprenticeship of Laura Ingalls Wilder," *South Dakota History* 13 (Winter 1983), 286.

2. *World Almanac and Book of Facts: 1992* (New York: Pharos, 1991), 310.

3. For complete citations of works discussed in this chapter, see Selected Bibliography.

4. See especially "People" in Chapter 3.

5. Pertinent to the mother-daughter collaboration are the following: Anderson, "The Literary Apprenticeship of Laura Ingalls Wilder" and "The Continuing Collaboration," 89–143; Fellman; Caroline Fraser, "The Prairie Queen," *New York Review of Books* (22 December 1994), 38, 40–45, hereafter cited as Fraser; Holtz, *Ghost*. See also Rosa Ann Moore, "Laura Ingalls Wilder's Orange Notebooks and the Art of the Little House Books," *Children's Literature* 4 (1975), 105–19; "The Little House Books: Rose-Colored Classics," *Children's Literature* 7 (1978), 7–16; and "Laura Ingalls Wilder and Rose Wilder Lane," *Children's Literature in Education* 11 (Autumn 1980).

6. I would add that the book of which we know Lane wrote a great deal—*Farmer Boy*—is, in my opinion, the weakest of the eight books. I have always found it more like *Let the Hurricane Roar* and *Free Land,* and less poetic and philosophical than any of the other seven books.

7. Fraser's example is Lane's *Let the Hurricane Roar,* which is about the same material that Wilder used in *On the Banks of Plum Creek.*

Notes and References

Chapter 3

1. Hamida Bosmajian, "Vastness and Contraction of Space in *Little House on the Prairie*," *Children's Literature* 11 (1983), 62.

2. Cited in note 17 to Chapter 1.

3. For a discussion of "basic trust" as the first developmental task, see Erik H. Erikson, *Insight and Responsibility* (New York: Norton, 1964).

4. Gaston Bachelard, *The Poetics of Reverie*, trans. Daniel Russell (Boston: Beacon, 1969); and *The Poetics of Space*, trans. Maria Jolas (Boston: Beacon, 1969); hereafter cited by title.

5. "Big Bad Wolf," *Children's Literature in Education* 17 (Summer 1988), 108.

6. Three excellent studies of gender roles in the *Little House* books are Anne Thompson Lee, "'It Is Better Farther On': Laura Ingalls Wilder and the Pioneer Spirit," *The Lion and the Unicorn* 3 (Spring 1979), 74–88; Elizabeth Segel, "Laura Ingalls Wilder's America: An Unflinching Assessment," *Children's Literature in Education* 8 (Summer 1977), 63–70; and Louise Mowder, "Domestication of Desire: Gender, Language, and Landscape in the Little House Books," *Children's Literature Association Quarterly* 17 (Spring 1992), 15–19. Hereafter cited by author's name.

7. Sandra L. Myers, *Westering Women: The Frontier Experience 1800–1915* (Albuquerque: University of New Mexico Press, 1982), 2–3; hereafter cited as Myers.

8. This development in the later *Little House* books foreshadows her agreement to marry Almanzo Wilder but not to obey him. For a discussion of the differences between "first wave" (1868–85) women such as Ma and "second wave" (1885–1930) women such as Laura, see Carol Fairbanks, *Pioneer Women: Images in American and Canadian Fiction* (New Haven, Conn.: Yale University Press, 1986); hereafter cited as Fairbanks. The "first wave" were reluctant and afraid and worked to bring about a settled life like the one they had left. The "second wave" felt at home on the prairie. They developed a relationship with and respect for the land, an intimacy that nurtured and transformed them (262–75).

9. Thich Nhat Hanh, *The Miracle of Mindfulness: A Manual on Meditation*, rev. ed. (Boston: Beacon, 1987), 11.

Chapter 4

1. See note 17 to Chapter 1.

2. This part of the chapter is from "The Magic Circle."

3. Delores Rosenblum, "'Intimate Immensity': Mythic Space in the Works of Laura Ingalls Wilder," in *Where the West Begins*, ed. Arthur R. Huseboe and William Geyer (Sioux Falls, S. Dak.: Center for Western Studies, 1978), 72–79.

4. I use "other" as a short way to refer to everyone and everything perceived as outside the self.

5. I am thankful to Ann Romines, "Preempting the Patriarch: The Problem of Pa's Stories in *Little House in the Big Woods,*" *Children's Literature Association Quarterly* 20 (Spring 1995), 15–18, for her insight about this major difference between *Little House in the Big Woods* and *Little House on the Prairie.* In Romines's words, "in order to create a series that would become a narrative of a girl's experience, Wilder and Lane had to preempt the patriarchal voice of their first two books. They began to discover their strategy in the third book, *Little House on the Prairie.* . . . [A]s the Little House leaves the Big Woods and hits the road West, it becomes the center of a mobile, exploratory, lyric *female* narrative" (18). Also useful for understanding the narrative technique in this novel is Charles Frey, "Laura and Pa: Family and Landscape in *Little House on the Prairie,*" *Children's Literature Association Quarterly* 12 (Fall 1987), 125–28, in which he describes "a fusion or confusion of child's and grown-up's points of view . . . early in the novel and never quite . . . overcome" (125).

6. See note 17 to Chapter 1.

7. Ralph Abraham, *Chaos—Gaia—Eros: A Chaos Pioneer Uncovers the Three Great Streams of History* (San Francisco: HarperCollins, 1994), 62.

8. Mircea Eliade, *Cosmos and History: The Myth of the Eternal Return,* trans. Willard R. Trask (New York: Harper and Row, 1949).

9. See Abraham's extensive bibliography, 239–52.

10. Paul Tillich, *Political Expectation* (New York: Harper and Row, 1971), 134.

Chapter 5

1. Joseph Campbell, with Bill Moyers, *The Power of Myth,* ed. Betty Sue Flowers (New York: Doubleday, 1988), 31; hereafter cited as *Power.*

2. I should again remind the reader of context—in particular, my personal context as a middle-aged, feminist scholar, grounded in literary criticism, myths, and theologies of the western world but having some acquaintance with myths and theologies of other cultures. In addition to being a professor of English, I am well on my way to a master of divinity degree in the Unitarian Universalist denomination. I am especially interested in comparative religion. I have also read examples and discussions of Native American mythology. Thus, although I can interpret only from my context, that context is broad and inclusive.

3. Joseph Campbell, *The Hero with a Thousand Faces* (New York: Pantheon, 1949); hereafter cited as *Hero.*

4. Evidence is abundant in all of Frye's work. He refers to the Bible; he uses Christian terms (for example, heaven and hell, death and resurrection);

and *The Great Code: The Bible and Literature* (New York: Harcourt Brace Jovanovich, 1982) and his title for his study of romance—*The Secular Scripture*—demonstrate his reliance on his Christian heritage. He does, however, bring in other cultural myths: for example, the goddess myths of the ancient near east, as described by Robert Graves in *The White Goddess: A Historical Grammar of Poetic Myth,* amended and enlarged (New York: Farrar, Straus, & Giroux, 1966).

5.   I rely principally on *Power* and *Hero*. In his search for universality, Campbell might be accused of ignoring his own context as a western scholar. Admittedly, we can never understand the myths of another culture as well as we can understand our own. Perhaps, though, we can understand them well enough to see what is wrong with ours, and how we might reinterpret Christianity for our own time or even seek a new, more beneficial myth.

6.   Many people associate the rise of patriarchy and the development of technology with the spread of Christianity. In fact, this is the underlying assumption of all the works cited in the notes to this chapter. Two studies which focus specifically on the connection are Elizabeth Dodson Gray, *Patriarchy as a Conceptual Trap* (Wellesley, Mass.: Roundtable Press, 1982); and Gerda Lerner, *The Creation of Patriarchy* (Oxford: Oxford University Press, 1986).

7.   For example, Paula Gunn Allen, *The Sacred Hoop: Recovering the Feminine in American Indian Traditions* (Boston: Beacon, 1986); Vine Deloria, Jr., *God Is Red* (New York: Grosset and Dunlap, 1973) and *The Metaphysics of Modern Existence* (San Francisco: Harper and Row, 1979); *Earth and Sky: Visions of the Cosmos in Native American Folklore,* ed. Ray A. Williams and Claire R. Farrar (Albuquerque: University of New Mexico Press, 1992); *I Become Part of It: Sacred Dimensions in Native American Life,* ed. D. M. Dooling and Paul Jordan-Smith (New York: Parabola, 1989); Sam D. Gill, *Mother Earth: An American Story* (Chicago: University of Chicago Press, 1987); Maureen Korp, *The Sacred Geography of the American Mound Builder* (Lewiston, N.Y.: Mellen, 1990); Belden C. Lane, *Landscapes of the Sacred: Geography and Narrative in American Spirituality* (New York: Paulist, 1988), especially chap. 2, "Seeking a Sacred Center: Places and Themes in Native American Spirituality"; James Swan, *Sacred Places: How the Living Earth Seeks Our Friendship* (Santa Fe, N.M.: Bear, 1990); George E. Tinker, "Native Americans and the Land: The End of Living, and the Beginning of Survival," in *Lift Every Voice: Constructing Christian Theologies from the Underside,* ed. Susan Brooks Thistlewaite and Mary Potter Engel (San Francisco: HarperCollins, 1990), 141–51; and Arthur Versluis, *Sacred Earth: The Spiritual Landscape of Native America* (Rochester, Vt.: Inter Traditions International, 1992), hereafter cited as Versluis.

8.   For example, Thomas Berry, *The Dream of the Earth* (San Francisco: Sierra Club Books, 1988); John B. Cobb and Herman E. Daly, *For*

the Common Good: Redirecting the Economy toward Community, the Environment, and a Sustainable Future (Boston: Beacon, 1989); Matthew Fox, *Original Blessing: A Primer in Creation Spirituality* (Santa Fe: Bear, 1983); John Hart, *The Spirit of the Earth: A Theology of the Land* (Mahwah, N.J.: Paulist, 1984); Dieter Hessel, ed., *After Nature's Revolt: Eco-Justice and Theology* (Minneapolis: Fortress, 1992); Carter Heyward, *Touching Our Strength: The Erotic as Power and the Love of God* (San Francisco: Harper and Row, 1989); Sallie McFague, *The Body of God: An Ecological Theology* (Minneapolis: Fortress, 1993); Judith Plant, ed., *Healing the Wounds: The Promise of Eco-Feminism* (Philadelphia: New Society, 1989). The best-known process theologian of the late twentieth century is Charles Hartshorne. See, for example, his *Omnipotence and Other Theological Mistakes* (Albany: State University of New York, 1984).

Others that are not quite Christian in their focus but are very important to me are Wendell Berry, *Home Economics* (Berkeley: North Point, 1987); Mary Daly, *Gyn/Ecology: The Metaphysics of Radical Feminism* (Boston: Beacon, 1979); G. Peter Fleck, *The Blessings of Imperfection: Reflections on the Mystery of Everyday Life* (Boston: Beacon, 1987); and Bill McKibben, *The End of Nature* (New York: Random House, 1989). Fleck (hereafter cited by name) is a Unitarian Universalist.

9. An early example of ecofeminism is Susan Griffin, *Woman and Nature: The Roaring Inside Her* (New York: Harper and Row, 1980). Other examples of feminist theologians, many of whom are ecofeminists, include Carter Heyward, Sallie McFague, and Judith Plant, cited in note 8; and Rosemary Radford Ruether, Elizabeth A. Johnson, Elizabeth Schussler Fiorenza, Mary Daly, Z. Budapest, Starhawk, Carol Christ, and Carolyn Merchant.

10. See Huston Smith, *The World's Religions* (San Francisco: HarperCollins, 1991); and Geoffrey Parrinder, ed., *World Religions: From Ancient History to the Present* (New York: Facts on File, 1971).

11. *Tao Te Ching: A New English Version with Foreword and Notes,* trans. Stephen Mitchell (New York: Harper and Row, 1988).

12. Cited in note 7 to this chapter. Of all the books I've read about Native American mythology, I rely most heavily on *Sacred Earth* because, like *Little House on the Prairie,* it focuses on the spiritual landscape of Kansas.

13. A book specifically about this view is Sallie McFague, *Metaphorical Theology: Models of God in Religious Language* (Philadelphia: Fortress, 1982). In the last chapter, McFague criticizes patriarchy for taking Christian metaphors literally, that is, for seeing God as male in gender and for using this as a reason for making females second-class citizens of the world and of heaven. Fundamentalists who take the Bible literally, of course, are the clearest example of those people who take metaphors for reality.

14. The material in this section was first explored in my articles "The Magic Circle of Laura Ingalls Wilder" and "The *Little House* Books: A Personal Story."

Chapter 6

1. See R. A. LeVine and Merry I. White, *Human Conditions: The Cultural Basis of Educational Development* (London: Routledge and Kegan Paul, 1986); and Elliot Turiel, *The Development of Social Knowledge: Morality and Convention* (New York: Cambridge University Press, 1983).

2. For the material on mythic thinking, I have relied heavily on Kieran Egan, *Primary Understanding: Education in Early Childhood* (New York: Routledge, 1988); hereafter cited as Egan.

3. As described, for example, by Nancy Chodorow, *The Reproduction of Mothering: Psychoanalysis and the Sociology of Gender* (Berkeley: University of California Press, 1978); William Damon, *The Moral Child: Nurturing Children's Natural Moral Growth* (New York: Free Press, 1988); Erik Erikson, *Childhood and Society* (New York: Norton, 1950); Sigmund Freud, *The Standard Edition of the Complete Psychological Works of Sigmund Freud*, ed. J. Strachey (London: Hogarth, 1953–74); Carol Gilligan, *In a Different Voice: Psychological Theory and Women's Development* (Cambridge: Harvard University Press, 1982); *Mapping the Moral Domain: A Contribution of Women's Thinking to Psychological Thinking and Education*, ed. Carol Gilligan, Janie Victoria Ward, and Jill McLean Taylor, with Betty Bardige (Cambridge: Harvard University Press, 1988); Jerome Kagan, *The Nature of the Child* (New York: Basic, 1984); Lawrence Kohlberg, *The Philosophy of Development: Moral Stages and the Idea of Justice: Essays on Moral Development*, vol. 1 (San Francisco: Harper and Row, 1981); Jean Piaget, *The Child's Conception of the World* (reprint of the 1929 original, Totowa, N.J.: Littlefield, Adams, 1979). Cited hereafter by author's name.

4. Richard Lansdown and Marjorie Walker, *Your Child's Development: From Birth through Adolescence* (New York: Knopf, 1991).

5. Sarah Gilead, "Emigrant Selves: Narrative Strategies in Three Women's Autobiographies," *Criticism* 30 (Winter 1988), 43; hereafter cited as Gilead.

6. Michael S. Pritchard, *On Becoming Responsible* (Lawrence: University Press of Kansas, 1991), 138–59.

7. For other examples, see Damon and Gilligan.

8. Jean Baker Miller, *Toward a New Psychology of Women*, 2d ed. (Boston: Beacon, 1986), 64.

9. Gary Paul Nabhan and Steven Trimble, *The Geography of Childhood: Why Children Need Wild Places* (Boston: Beacon, 1994), 61–75.

10. Julia T. Wood, *Who Cares? Women, Care, and Culture* (Carbondale: Southern Illinois University Press, 1994), 33–61.

11. Anne MacLeod, "The *Caddie Woodlawn* Syndrome: American Girlhood in the Nineteenth Century," in *A Century of Childhood: 1820–1920,* ed. Mary Lynn Stevens Heininger, Karin Calvert, Barbara Finkelstein, Kathy Vandell, Anne Scott MacLeod, and Harvey Green (Rochester, N.Y.: Margaret Woodbury Strong Museum, 1984), 98–119.

Chapter 7

1. Frederick Turner, *Beyond Geography: The Western Spirit against the Wilderness* (New York: Viking, 1980).

2. Yi-Fu Tuan, *Landscapes of Fear* (New York: Pantheon, 1979).

3. See Hoxie Neale Fairchild, *The Noble Savage: A Study in Romantic Naturalism* (New York: Russell and Russell, 1955); and Roy Harvey Pearce, *The Savages of America* (Baltimore: John Hopkins University Press, 1953).

4. See R. W. B. Lewis, cited in note 17 to Chapter 1.

5. As several newspaper pieces reprinted in *Little House in the Ozarks* reveal, Wilder opposed reckless destruction and waste of the environment (47–50, 69–70, 76–77, 87–90, 255–56, and 282–84, for example).

6. Some of the columns collected in *Little House in the Ozarks* argue for simplicity and sustainability; see, for example, "The March of Progress" (30–33), "Sweet Williams" (51–52), and "The Things That Matter" (311–12).

7. John Cobb and Herbert Daly, *For the Common Good: Redirecting the Economy toward Community, the Environment, and a Sustainable Future* (Boston: Beacon, 1989).

8. See Ihab Hassan, *Radical Innocence,* cited in note 17 to Chapter 1.

9. Writers tend to rely heavily on their personal experience and often tell the story of their respective growing up experiences. See Jerome Hamilton, *Seasons of Youth: The Bildungsroman from Dickens to Golding* (Cambridge: Harvard University Press, 1974). On the use of the artist as hero in fiction, see Maurice Beebe, *Ivory Towers and Sacred Founts: The Artist as Hero in Fiction from Goethe to Joyce* (New York: New York University Press, 1964). For an explanation of why writers often make artists their heroes, see Herbert Read, *Art and Alienation: The Role of the Artist in Society* (New York: Horizon, 1967).

10. Alexis de Tocqueville may have been the first to recognize that pantheism would become an important spiritual impulse; see volume II of *Democracy in America,* especially 31–32. As the idea of wilderness changed with the emergence of romanticism, our writers (Emerson, Thoreau, and Whitman, for example) celebrated nature as a mystical contact with divinity.

They first expressed the distinctive American love of wilderness—a love that has led us to deify nature even as we destroy it.

Appendix

1.   Unless otherwise noted, the following are cited hereafter by author's name. See Laura Rozakis, *Laura Ingalls Wilder: Activities Based on Research from the Laura Ingalls Wilder Homes and Museums* (New York: Scholastic Professional Books, 1993); *Laura Ingalls Wilder and Rose Wilder Lane: 1937–1939* (West Branch, Iowa: Education Programs, Herbert Hoover Presidential Library, 1992), hereafter cited as *LIW-RWL;* Olive Stafford Niles, Helen Mitchell Popp, and Sara Throop, *Little House on the Prairie Teacher's Guide and Activity Packet,* Literature Enrichment Ideas for Paperbacks (Littleton, Mass.: Sundance, 1991); Christine Olivieri Hacket, *Little House in the Classroom: A Guide to Using the Laura Ingalls Wilder Books* (Carthage, Ill.: Good Apple, 1989); Anne Troy and Phyllis Green, *Little House on the Prairie* (Palatine, Ill.: Novel Units, 1987); *Laura Ingalls Wilder,* Porta-Center (Phoenix, Ariz.: Thinking Caps, 1980), cited as Porta-Center. For cooking in the *Little House* books, see Barbara Walker, *The Little House Cookbook: Frontier Foods from Laura Ingalls Wilder's Classic Stories* (New York: Harper and Row, 1979). For the music and words of songs played and sung in the books, see Eugenia Garson, *The Laura Ingalls Wilder Songbook* (New York: Harper and Row, 1968).

2.   See Jim Trelease, *The New Read-Aloud Handbook* (New York: Penguin, 1989).

3.   Laura Ingalls Wilder, *Little House on the Prairie—Premiere Movie,* produced and directed by Michael Landon, John Hawkins, and William Claxton, 120 min.; NBC Production with Ed Friendly, 1989, videocassette.

4.   The following are written for children: William Anderson, *A Biography of Laura Ingalls Wilder* (New York: HarperCollins, 1992); *Laura Wilder of Mansfield* (De Smet, S. Dak.: Laura Ingalls Wilder Memorial Society, 1982); Glenda Blair, *Laura Ingalls Wilder* (New York: Putnam, 1981); Patricia Reilly Giff, *Laura Ingalls Wilder: Growing Up in the Little House* (New York: Viking Kestrel, 1987); Carol Greene, *Laura Ingalls Wilder: Author of the Little House Books* (Chicago: Children's Press, 1990); Kathryn Lasky and Meribah Knight, *Searching for Laura Ingalls: A Reader's Journey* (New York: Macmillan, 1993); Irene V. Lichty, *The Ingalls Family from Plum Creek to Walnut Grove via Burr Oak, Iowa* (Mansfield, Mo.: Laura Ingalls Wilder Memorial Society, 1970); Roger Lea MacBride, *Little House on Rocky Ridge* (New York: HarperCollins, 1993); and Megan Stine, *The Story of Laura Ingalls Wilder; Pioneer Girl* (New York: Dell, 1992). Holtz's and Zochert's books are for adults but might be read by any skilled sixth-grader.

5.   This is Laurie Rozakis's idea; see page 56, where she supplies a manuscript version of the first page of "The Hard Winter" and asks students to compare it with pages 1 and 2 of *The Long Winter*.

6.   Harvey Brett, *Cassie's Journey: Going West in the 1860's* (New York: Holiday House, 1988); George and Ellen Laycock, *How the Settlers Lived* (New York: McKay, 1980); Conrad R. Stein, *The Story of the Homestead Act* (New York: Children's Press, 1978); Russell Friedman, *Indian Chiefs* (New York: Holiday House, 1987); Frank W. Porter III, ed., *Indians of North America* (New York: Chelsea House)—see especially Frank W. Porter, *The Cherokee* (1989) and Terry P. Wilson, *The Osage* (1988).

7.   Margaret Mackey, "Growing with Laura: Time, Space, and the Reader in the 'Little House' Books," *Children's Literature in Education* 23 (June 1992), 59–74, provides insights into how the treatment of time and space become increasingly complex as Laura and the implied reader age.

Selected Bibliography

Primary Sources

The *Little House* Books

Little House in the Big Woods. New York: Harper, 1932. Reissued with new illustrations by Garth Williams, 1953. Reprint. New York: Harper Trophy (paperback), 1971; cited as *LHBW*.

Farmer Boy. New York: Harper, 1933. Reissued with new illustrations by Garth Williams, 1953. Reprint. New York: Harper Trophy (paperback), 1971; cited as *FB*.

Little House on the Prairie. New York: Harper, 1935. Reissued with new illustrations by Garth Williams, 1953. Reprint. New York: Harper Trophy (paperback), 1971; cited as *LHP*.

On the Banks of Plum Creek. New York, Harper, 1937. Reissued with new illustrations by Garth Williams, 1953. Reprint. New York: Harper Trophy (paperback), 1971; cited as *OBPC*.

By the Shores of Silver Lake. New York: Harper, 1939. Reissued with new illustrations by Garth Williams, 1953. Reprint. New York: Harper Trophy (paperback), 1971; cited as *BSSL*.

The Long Winter. New York: Harper, 1940. Reissued with new illustrations by Garth Williams, 1953. Reprint. New York: Harper Trophy (paperback), 1971; cited as *LW*.

Little Town on the Prairie. New York: Harper, 1941. Reissued with new illustrations by Garth Williams, 1953. Reprint. New York: Harper Trophy (paperback), 1971; cited as *LTP*.

These Happy Golden Years. New York: Harper, 1943. Reissued with new illustrations by Garth Williams, 1953. Reprint. New York: Harper Trophy (paperback), 1971; cited as *THGY*.

The First Four Years. New York: Harper, 1971. Reprint. New York: Harper Trophy (paperback), 1971.

Published Diaries and Correspondence

On the Way Home: The Diary of a Trip from South Dakota in Mansfield, Missouri, in 1894. With a setting by Rose Wilder Lane. New York: Harper, 1962. Reprint. New York: Harper Trophy (paperback), 1976.

West from Home: Letters of Laura Ingalls Wilder, San Francisco, 1915. Edited by Roger Lea MacBride. New York: Harper, 1974. Reprint. New York: Harper Trophy (paperback), 1976.

Articles and Excerpts

A Little House Sampler: Laura Ingalls Wilder and Rose Wilder Lane. Edited by William T. Anderson. Lincoln: University of Nebraska Press, 1988; cited as *LHS.*

Little House in the Ozarks. Edited by Stephen Hines. Nashville: Thomas Nelson, 1991.

Research Collections

Herbert Hoover Presidential Library, West Branch, Iowa. Rose Wilder Lane papers, manuscripts, extensive correspondence.

University of Missouri. Manuscripts, some correspondence.

Laura Ingalls Wilder Memorial Society. All the *Little House* sites and Wilder's home in Mansfield, Missouri, have been preserved or re-created. The most extensive collections are in Mansfield, Missouri, and De Smet, South Dakota. Two of the Memorial Societies produce newsletters: *Notes from Laura Ingalls Wilder Memorial Society, Inc.,* in Pepin, Wisconsin, and *Laura Ingalls Wilder Lore* in De Smet, South Dakota.

Secondary Sources

Biographical Works

Anderson, William T. *A Biography of Laura Ingalls Wilder.* New York: HarperCollins, 1992.

———. *Laura Ingalls Wilder Country: The People and the Places in Laura Ingalls Wilder's Life and Books.* Photographs by Leslie A. Kelly. New York: HarperPerennial, 1990. An edition of this book was published in Japan by Kyuryudo Art Publishing in 1988.

Selected Bibliography

——. *Laura Wilder of Mansfield*. De Smet, S. Dak.: Laura Ingalls Wilder Memorial Society, 1982.

——. *The Story of the Ingalls*. 7th ed. De Smet, S. Dak.: Laura Ingalls Wilder Memorial Society, 1982.

——. *Laura's Rose*. De Smet, S. Dak.: Laura Ingalls Wilder Memorial Society, 1976.

Blair, Glenda. *Laura Ingalls Wilder*. New York: Putnam, 1981.

Giff, Patricia Reilly. *Laura Ingalls Wilder: Growing Up in the Little House*. New York: Viking Kestrel, 1987.

Greene, Carol. *Laura Ingalls Wilder: Author of the Little House Books*. Chicago: Children's Press, 1990.

Holtz, William. *The Ghost in the Little House: A Life of Rose Wilder Lane*. Columbia: University of Missouri Press, 1993.

Lasky, Kathryn and Meribah Knight. *Searching for Laura Ingalls: A Reader's Journey*. New York: Macmillan, 1993.

Lichty, Irene V. *The Ingalls Family from Plum Creek to Walnut Grove via Burr Oak, Iowa*. Mansfield, Mo.: Laura Ingalls Wilder Memorial Society, 1970.

MacBride, Roger Lea. *Little House on Rocky Ridge*. New York: HarperCollins, 1993.

Zochert, Donald. *Laura: The Life of Laura Ingalls Wilder*. Chicago: Regnery, 1976.

Teaching Resources

Eddins, Doris K. *A Teacher's Tribute to Laura Ingalls Wilder*. Washington, D.C.: Department of Elementary School Principals, National Education Association, 1967.

Garson, Eugenia. *The Laura Ingalls Wilder Songbook*. New York: Harper and Row, 1968.

Hackett, Christine Olivieri. *Little House in the Classroom: A Guide to Using the Laura Ingalls Wilder Books*. Carthage, Ill.: Good Apple, 1989.

Laura Ingalls Wilder and Rose Wilder Lane. West Branch, Iowa: Education Programs, Herbert Hoover Presidential Library, 1992.

Niles, Olive Stafford, Helen Mitchell Popp, and Sara Throop, eds. "Little House on the Prairie." *Literature Activities for Paperbacks*. Littleton, Mass.: Sundance, 1991.

Porta-Center #224. *Laura Ingalls Wilder*. Phoenix, Ariz.: Thinking Caps Materials for the Gifted, 1980.

Rozakis, Laurie. *Laura Ingalls Wilder: Activities Based on Research from the Laura Ingalls Wilder Homes and Museums*. New York: Scholastic Professional Books, 1993.

Troy, Ann Green, and Phyllis Green. *Little House on the Prairie.* Palatine, Ill.: Novel Units, 1987.

Walker, Barbara. *The Little House Cookbook: Frontier Foods from Laura Ingalls Wilder's Classic Stories.* Illustrated by Garth Williams. New York: Harper and Row, 1979.

Literary Studies

Anderson, William T. "Laura Ingalls Wilder and Rose Wilder Lane: The Continuing Collaboration." *South Dakota History* 16 (Summer 1986), 89–143. Continues the study begun in "The Literary Apprenticeship" through the creation of *Farmer Boy* and Lane's writing of *Let the Hurricane Roar,* using material from her mother's life.

———. "The Literary Apprenticeship of Laura Ingalls Wilder." *South Dakota History* 13 (1983), 285–331. Traces the development of Wilder's writing for newspapers and magazines through "Pioneer Girl" and *Little House in the Big Woods,* increasingly under her daughter's guidance.

Arnold, Arthur. "Big Bad Wolf." *Children's Literature in Education* 17 (Summer 1986), 101–11. Criticizes Wilder's portrait of the wolves in *Little House on the Prairie* as similar to her portrait of Native Americans and revealing her lack of understanding of either.

Barker, Roger G. "The Influence of Frontier Environments on Behavior." In *The American West: New Perspectives, New Dimensions,* ed. Jerome O. Steffen, 61–93. Norman: University of Oklahoma Press, 1979. Analyzes the *Little House* books in terms of their reflection of frontier moral values.

Bosmajian, Hamida. "Vastness and Contraction of Space in *Little House on the Prairie.*" *Children's Literature* 11 (1983), 49–63. Approaches the novel from a phenomenological viewpoint.

Erisman, Fred. "Laura Ingalls Wilder, 1867–1957." In *Writers for Children: Critical Studies of Major Authors since the Seventeenth Century,* ed. Jane Bingham, 617–23. New York: Scribner, 1988. Summarizes Wilder's career and accomplishments as the writer of the *Little House* books.

———. "Regionalism in American Children's Literature." In *Society and Children's Literature,* ed. James H. Fraser, 53–75. Boston: Godine, 1978. Discusses the extent to which regionalism has characterized children's literature, focusing heavily on Wilder's work.

———. "The Regional Vision of Laura Ingalls Wilder." In *Studies in Medieval, Renaissance, American Literature: A Festschrift,* ed. Betsy Feagan Colquitt, 165–71. Fort Worth: Texas Christian University Press, 1971. Looks at the *Little House* books as regionalism.

Fellman, Anita Claire. "Laura Ingalls Wilder and Rose Wilder Lane: The Politics of a Mother-Daughter Relationship." *Signs* 15 (Spring 1990),

535–61. Argues that Lane developed her extreme political views (libertarianism) as a result of maternal deprivation and of working with her mother on the *Little House* books, which embody an extreme individualism mother and daughter eventually shared.

Fraser, Caroline. "The Prairie Queen." *New York Review of Books* (22 December 1994), 38, 40–45. Reviews *The Ghost in the Little House, The First Four Years, A Little House Sampler,* and *West from Home: Letters of Laura Ingalls Wilder, San Francisco, 1915.*

Frey, Charles. "Laura and Pa: Family and Landscape in *Little House on the Prairie.*" *Children's Literature Quarterly* 12 (Fall 1987), 125–28. Examines the fusion of Laura and Pa and the prairie resulting from Wilder's use of a child's point of view (that is, one lacking clear boundaries and possessing great energy and imagination) and conveying a "deep, deep affection for the life of all being" (128).

Gates, Catherine. "Image, Imagination, and Initiation: Teaching as a Rite of Passage in the Novels of L. M. Montgomery and Laura Ingalls Wilder." *Children's Literature in Education* 20 (September 1989), 165–73. Examines the relationship between Laura's decision to teach and her passage in adulthood.

Gilead, Sarah. "Emigrant Selves: Narrative Strategies in Three Women's Autobiographies." *Criticism* 30 (Winter 1988), 43–62. Shows that as Laura matures, she replaces her emigrant self as a traveler in love with wilderness with a socialized or civilized self, but that in the books she eventually wrote she preserved the early self.

Holtz, William. "Closing the Circle: The American Optimism of Laura Ingalls Wilder." *Great Plains Quarterly* 4 (1984), 79–90. Points out that a different kind of farming was demanded by the great plains west of 100th meridian; Wilder's father and husband were not prepared for this and were therefore defeated. This is at odds with the tone of the *Little House* books.

Horn Book Magazine (December 1953) (special issue on Wilder), 413–39. Reprint. Contains several articles, including Garth Williams, "Illustrating the Little House Books"; Virginia Kirkus, "Discovering Laura Ingalls Wilder"; and "A Letter from Laura Ingalls Wilder."

Jacobs, William. "Frontier Faith Revisited: The Little House Books of Laura Ingalls Wilder." *Horn Book Magazine* 66 (1965), 465–73. Traces what he sees as frontier moral values in the *Little House* books.

Lee, Anna Thompson. "'It Is Better Farther On': Laura Ingalls Wilder and the Pioneer Spirit." *The Lion and the Unicorn* 3 (1979), 74–88. Explores Laura's growing perception of Ma and Pa and shows that both are portrayed as complex.

Mackey, Margaret. "Growing with Laura: Time, Space, and the Reader in the 'Little House' Books." *Children's Literature in Education* 23 (June

1992), 59–74. Shows how Wilder's treatment of time and space become increasingly complex as Laura and the implied reader age.

Miller, John E. *Laura Ingalls Wilder's Little Town: Where History and Literature Meet.* Lawrence: University of Kansas Press, 1993. Examines the correspondence between Wilder's books and the historical record and analyzes the extent to which narrative technique required a "stripped-down history" (5).

Moore, Rosa Ann. "Laura Ingalls Wilder and Rose Wilder Lane: The Chemistry of Collaboration." *Children's Literature in Education* 11 (1980), 101–9. Using the mother-daughter correspondence about *By the Shores of Silver Lake,* identifies specific ways in which Lane influenced the book.

———. "The Little House Books: Rose-Colored Classics." *Children's Literature* 7 (1978), 7–16. Examines Rose Wilder Lane's papers regarding the *Little House* books, including manuscripts and correspondence, to trace Lane's function as her mother's editor and agent.

———. "Laura Ingalls Wilder's Orange Notebooks and the Art of the Little House Books." *Children's Literature* 4 (1975), 105–19. Compares passages about the same incidents in *The First Four Years* and *These Happy Golden Years,* both published and manuscript versions, and concludes that Wilder was a skilled editor.

Mowder, Louise. "Domestication of Desire: Gender, Language, and Landscape in the Little House Books." *Children's Literature Association Quarterly* 17 (Spring 1992), 15–19. Argues that the wilderness in these books is masculine and childish rather than feminine, and that women tame the wilderness—turning the usual American myth upside down.

Romines, Ann. "Preempting the Patriarch: The Problem of Pa's Stories in *Little House in the Big Woods.*" *Children's Literature Association Quarterly* 20 (Spring 1995), 15–18. Suggests that Wilder's first and second novels are less interesting than her third and later novels because these two are controlled, respectively, by Pa's and Almanzo's viewpoints, and all the later ones are told much more clearly by Laura as a child.

Rosenblum, Delores. "'Intimate Immensity': Mythic Space in the Works of Laura Ingalls Wilder." In *Where the West Begins,* ed. Arthur R. Juseboe and William Gever, 72–79. Sioux Falls, S. Dak.: Center for Western Studies, 1978. Analyzes the *Little House* books using Gaston Bachelard's *The Poetics of Space.*

Segel, Elizabeth. "Laura Ingalls Wilder's America: An Unflinching Assessment." *Children's Literature in Education* 8 (1977), 63–70. Examines *Little House on the Prairie* in terms of its complex treatment of gender roles and racial attitudes.

Selected Bibliography

Spaeth, Janet. *Laura Ingalls Wilder*. Twayne's United States Authors Series: Children's Literature. New York: Twayne, 1987. Offers chapters on Wilder's life, her use of folklore, pioneering in the books, her feminism, how the language and content of the books reflect Laura's growing up, Almanzo's life, and Wilder's fascination with the various ways experience can be seen and written about.

Susina, Jan. "The Voices of the Prairie: The Use of Music in Laura Ingalls Wilder's *Little House on the Prairie*." *The Lion and the Unicorn* 16 (December 1992), 158–66. Analyzes the auditory imagery of the novel, to show that human and natural music combine in harmony to suggest that the prairie is an earthly paradise.

Whitaker, Muriel. "Perceiving Prairie Landscape: The Young Person's View of a Western Frontier." *Children's Literature Association Quarterly* 8 (Winter 1983), 30–32. Suggests that the prairie in the *Little House* books is used as an "earthy paradise" (30).

Wolf, Virginia L. "Laura Ingalls Wilder's *Little House* Books: A Personal Story." In *Touchstones: Reflections on the Best in Children's Literature*, ed. Perry Nodelman, vol. 1, 291–300. West Lafayette, Ind.: Children's Literature Association, 1985. Argues that the *Little House* books are fundamentally about Laura's maturation and that any one book must be analyzed in the context of the series.

———. "The Magic Circle of Laura Ingalls Wilder." *Children's Literature Association Quarterly* 10 (Winter 1985), 168–70. Explores Wilder's use of the circle as a symbolic image and a structural device in individual *Little House* books and in the series as a whole.

———. "The Symbolic Center: *Little House in the Big Woods*." *Children's Literature in Education* 13 (1982), 107–14. Analyzes the style and structure of the novel to determine its creation of a mythic center in the little house, a place that vivifies the world and provides psychic balance.

Index

163

Index

Individualism, 17–18, 19–20
"Influence of Frontier Environments on Behavior" (Barker), 26
Ingalls, Carrie, 46
Ingalls, Laura (character), 46–50, 78–79; binary opposites and, 92–93; boundaries of, 92; development as a writer, 100–103; gender development of, 97–99, 100; innocence of, 116, 117–18; moral development of, 97–99; mythic thinking of, 91–92; papoose and, 52, 53, 57, 58; primitivism of, 105; psychosocial development of, 94–97; search for identity by, 122–23; as seer and artist, 124–26. *See also* Wilder, Laura Ingalls (author)
Ingalls, "Ma," 45–46, 119–20; china figurine possession of, 53; conservatism of, 70; relationship with Pa, 118, 120
Ingalls, Mary, 46
Ingalls, "Pa," 50–51; attitude toward nature, 81–82; fiddle, 52, 53; primitivism of, 105; relationship with Ma, 118, 120; as teacher, 81; wilderness and, 106
Innocence, 115–20
"Intimate Immensity" (Rosenblum), 25

Jacobs, William, "Frontier Faith Revisited," 26
Journey, mythic idea of, 86

Kansas, Native American reservations in, 12
Kirkus, Virginia, 23

Lane, Rose Wilder, 14; conservatism of, 16–17; role in creation of *Little House* books, 28–32
"Laura and Pa: Family and Landscapes" (Frey), 25
Laura Ingalls Wilder (Spaeth), 24, 26, 28
"Laura Ingalls Wilder and the Pioneer Spirit" (Segel), 26
Laura Ingalls Wilder's Little Town: Where History and Literature Meet (Miller), 23–24
Lines, 68–69
Little House books: circulation of, 22; form of, 27–28; intended readers, 27–28; versus "Little House on the Prairie" television show, 22; titles of, 62
Little House in the Big Woods, 6, 15, 50, 62, 122–23; "attractors" in, 67; binary opposites in, 93; compared with *Little House on the Prairie*, 55–56, 59; Laura's psychosocial development in, 94; Rose Wilder Lane's role in creation of, 30; technology in, 111; title of, 61–62
Little House on the Prairie, 6, 8, 50, 62; "attractors" in, 67; binary opposites in, 93; chaos in, 70–71; child's viewpoint in, 78–79; Christianity in, 73; compared with *Little House in the Big Woods*, 55–56, 59; description of pioneer life in, 25; initial reviews of, 22–23; Laura's psychosocial development in, 94; Laura's view of Native Americans in, 47–48; manifest destiny in, 68–69; mythic journey in, 85, 86; nature and art in, 107, 108;

165

Index

The Author

Virginia L. Wolf received her B.S. (English Education), M.A., and Ph.D. in English from the University of Kansas. She is professor of English at the University of Wisconsin-Stout and author of *Louise Fitzhugh, Changing the Climate of the College Classroom,* and about 50 articles on the children's novel. She has held various leadership roles in the Children's Literature Association (ChLA), including being president, and has delivered papers at conferences of ChLA, the Modern Language Association (MLA), various regional divisions of the MLA, the National Council of Teachers of English, and elsewhere. Currently, she is also a candidate for a master of divinity degree at United Theological Seminary.